The History of
Wildlife in
America

Library of Congress CIP Data: page 205

"Hunting of the Grizzly Bear" by Karl Bodmer, 1842.

The History of
Wildlife in America

By Hal Borland

NATIONAL WILDLIFE FEDERATION

Contents

1. *Turdus Melodus*, Wood Thrush. 2. *Turdus Migratorius*, Redbreasted Thrush, or Robin.
3. *Sitta Carolinensis*, White breasted black-capped Nuthatch. 4. *Sitta Varia*, Red-bellied black-capped Nuthatch.

Introduction

Our destination was Hell's Canyon. In Arizona where I grew up a half-century ago, that name was as familiar as Main Street was in the East but still it struck an ominous chord in my 11-year-old mind.

This was my first real pack trip and camp-out, though my home was near the Tonto National Forest whose mountains and canyons then teemed with wild animals. The invitation to ride into this vast, mysterious land had come from the supervisor of the forest who by great good fortune happened to be a neighbor. Feeding my speculations of the wild animals of the area were the novels of Zane Grey; I had just finished reading his *Under the Tonto Rim*, set in the very forest we were to visit.

As we pitched our tent in the Mogollon Mountains the first night out, I began to hear the night sounds ascribed by Zane Grey to the creatures of the Southwest. Then I lay down and tried to sleep. But every nearby rustle made me think of the Rim's storied grizzly, Old Silver Tip. The more I listened the more certain I became that *he* was out there. My only question was when and how he would strike.

Of course Silver Tip and all of his kind were staying well away from our campfire that night. And I soon forgot about that legendary bear. But the questions about wildlife, what it would do in a given situation and why, persisted. It was a source of great pleasure for me, as I grew, to discover some of the answers. Since I was urged by my family to follow a career of public service in work that I would enjoy, it seemed natural that I wound up in the science of wildlife management.

Now, after 40 years in the field and in related wildlife affairs, I do indeed feel grateful for that early, formative adventure and for the focusing of my career on wildlife. Yet I strongly feel that *all* Americans should have an opportunity to perceive and appreciate their wildlife heritage. If not by means of personal experience such as I have been recalling, then by a graphic and informative book in which they could be brought face to face with the extraordinary and unique animals that are the natural lords of North America. With those thoughts on my mind, I turned to the National Wildlife Federation's editors, asking them to produce a popular, illustrated book in time for the bicentennial celebrations. This handsome volume is the result.

It has been a special joy for us in the course of this work to enter into a partnership with author Hal Borland, one of America's most respected nature writers. Hal, known to a wide audience both for his books and for his essays on the editorial page of the *New York Times*, brings a wealth of experience to the task of chronicling outdoor America. He knows the land and frontier life, having been born in Nebraska and having grown up in Colorado. There he helped his father build a sod house and his family struggled to make good on their homesteader's claim. Today Hal lives in rural Connecticut, where deer munch his apples in the fall and pollution dirties the river at the bottom of the field. He remains remarkably attuned to the land, remarkably able to tune others in as well.

Perhaps the greatest surprise to me as Hal's text took shape was that his narrative was completely different from a mere history of the United States with animals mentioned here and there in appropriate spots. Instead, it gives an exciting new view of the American panorama. We see the animals as a constant presence, helping the American people, first to survive, and then to understand and to enjoy life in this new land.

In the colonial era the deer and the cod gave our first settlers their food, their clothes, and their fertilizer (once we'd learned the Indians' lessons); in the early national era the beaver and the buffalo (which we will never learn to call properly the bison) helped lead our westering ancestors up the rivers and across the plains to the Rockies. More recently such diverse animals as the rare pupfish and the southern bald eagle, by their very imperilment, have helped us see the necessity for conserving not only our wilderness resources for them, but all resources for our own future needs. At this very moment scientists in the field are watching the condor and monitoring the wolf with an eye to our mutual survival. We are rediscovering what our forefathers knew, that we can learn much from wildlife about living on this continent.

Another historic gift of the American animals to the American people has been sheer beauty. This beauty has been preserved through the artworks of American painter-naturalists. But how to present adequately in our book the great works of such wildlife artists as John White (grandfather of the Lost Colony's Virginia Dare) and John J. Audubon? Or how to do justice to the extensive paintings of the later frontier artists, Karl Bodmer, Titian Peale, and George Catlin? Or what place to give to the works of American Indians and present-day color photographers? The editors met that vast challenge by designing six special portfolios appropriate to the respective chapters of this book. Each is a gallery of American treasures, and each is also a lively place to wander, full of the sounds of the birds and the trumpeting of the elk. My advice to the reader is to take his time as he passes through.

Heroes in buckskin and modern dress throng the pages of both text and portfolio—from the distant figures of Meriwether Lewis and William Clark to the twentieth century crusaders "Ding" Darling (who founded the National Wildlife Federation), Aldo Leopold, and Rachel Carson. The colonial naturalist John Bartram speaks to us across the years as do the conservationist John Muir and the political dynamo Theodore Roosevelt. Though their names and even their faces may be familiar, we have yet to recognize them as important as generals, as historically significant as statesmen. Yet that is the measure of them in this book with its refreshingly different view of American history.

Perhaps the one quality this diverse group of writers and scientists and painters and stalkers possess in common is this: like the mountain men of yore, they loved what they were doing. And that, I must admit, is an unusual aspect of American leadership. But only that explains the dedication of Alexander Wilson when he decided in 1806 to paint and describe every bird in America, and only that accounts for the determination of Enos Mills at the turn of the last century to save forever a part of the Colorado Rockies as a national park. Only that kind of zeal explains the peculiarly American, organizational passion of the citizen-conservationists who have enrolled in the ranks of wildlife groups—3,500,000 in the National Wildlife Federation alone.

Scientists and layman alike, they are deeply devoted to the wildlife cause, and they see pragmatic evidence that by working together something can be done. Hal Borland notes the return of the deer to his Connecticut hillside pastures; headlines tell that the whooping cranes' eggs have successfully hatched. It's happening.

Thus the hero of the hour, the wildlife professional who stands at the center of the planning team or chairs the environmental task force, is already helping to write the next chapter of wildlife history. Behind him in this book march rank upon rank of Americans who have felt or reasoned or acted on behalf of wildlife. Their story has been a changing one, developing with the needs and concepts of the eras. But as an ongoing search for harmony in a vital, mutually enriching relationship, it is nonetheless coherent and consistent.

We salute all members of the wildlife fraternity for what they will yet do in defense of the land and its life. And we hail those who have gone before. There is a history of wildlife in America, and it belongs to us all.

Thomas L. Kimball
Executive Vice President
National Wildlife Federation

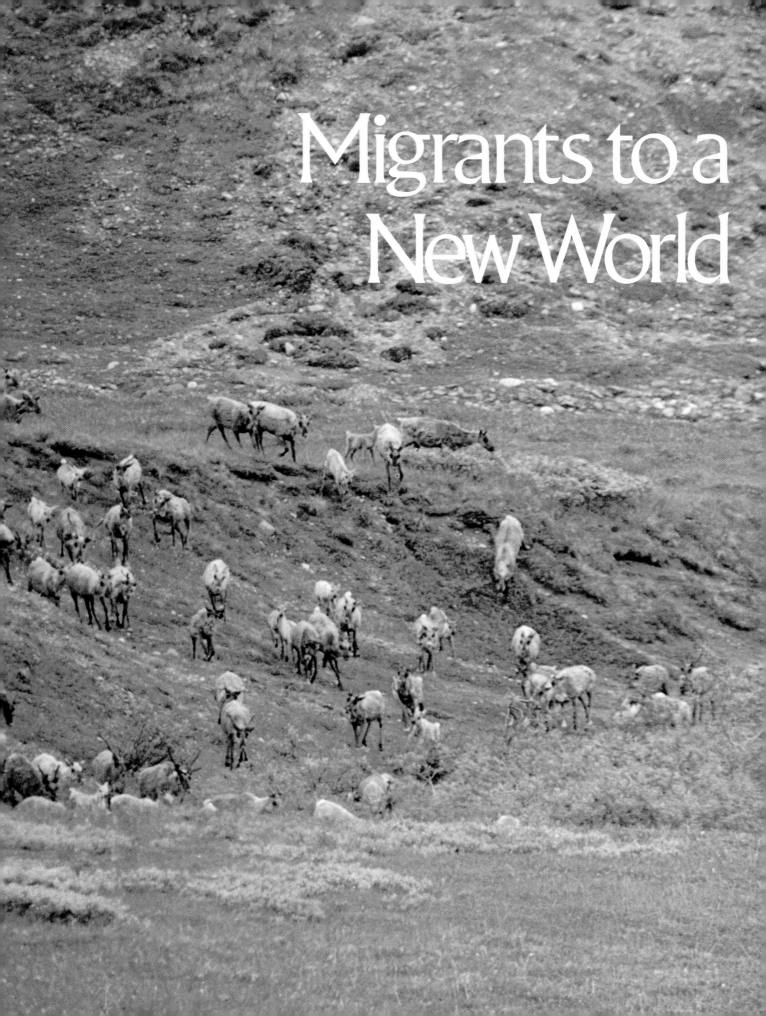

Migrants to a
New World

The herds of caribou and long-horned bison grazed east, always east, as though each day's rising sun beckoned them. When the big wolves or the saber-tooth cats attacked them, as they did almost every day, the herds fled eastward through the tall marsh grass and the willow brush. The musk oxen and the shaggy mammoths, big as elephants, and the huge cave bears that harried and fed on them, constantly moved eastward, too, but more slowly. It was almost as though the turning earth, west to east, was forcing them to move east or be spun off to oblivion. But the grass was lush and the low bushes full of leafage; and the lushness stretched to the horizon except to the north. To the north were banks of gray fog, and beyond the fog was the Big Ice, the mile-thick glaciers of the last Ice Age.

Behind the herds and the wolves and bears and cats came the hunters, a small tribe of them. The men were dark-haired, sinewy, and armed with flint-pointed spears. The women were muscular, broad-hipped, and hunched under their packs of primitive cooking gear and robes for bedding. Most of them had babies in arms or perched on their packs. Half-grown children romped or plodded, boys striding like men, brandishing poles for spears, girls carrying packs. They followed the herds and had no fixed home. Long ago, those before them had come north out of Africa into Asia. There some of those ancient ones turned west at the foot of the Big Ice and eventually reached Europe and were called Cro-Magnons. Others turned east, as this party, following the herds like the other predators.

That was the way of life: first the green of the leaf, the chlorophyll, which made the basic food, the starch and sugar, from sun and air and water; then the grazers and the browsers, which ate the leaves and converted the starch into meat; and then the meat-eaters, the predators, four-footed and two-footed. Among the latter came this small tribe of hunters following the herds eastward, toward America.

They had no way of knowing the Big Ice was part of the great ice sheet that covered much of the northern hemisphere or that it locked up so much of the earth's water that the oceans were lowered 250 feet or more and uncovered a land bridge almost 1,000 miles wide between Siberia and Alaska. For

Mighty mammals ruled North America in the Pleistocene Epoch, 2,500,000 to 10,000 years ago. The saber-tooth cat (opposite) stalked camel, ground sloth, long-horned bison, and even the 13-foot-high mammoth (skeleton above). Then it pounced and, gripping with powerful claws, stabbed its prey with serrated seven-inch canine teeth. With the arrival of weapon-wielding man (top) and changing climate, these gigantic beasts died out.

thousands of years the land bridge was a grassy, brushy lowland on which herds and flocks and family groups of animals had crossed from Asia to America. It led to a corridor of more pasturage and streams of sweet water along the west coast of North America. Two-way traffic on this land bridge enriched the wildlife populations of both continents just as a tropical land bridge far to the south, the Isthmus of Panama, enabled wildlife to move to and fro between North and South America.

The wildlife of this open and verdant continent, and the way it has shared this North America with man from the Ice Age till today, has never been fully appreciated. To name and portray the major species, to describe their behavior and (most important) their significance to us in different generations of American life—that is the purpose of this book. We shall see and hear and almost feel and smell countless herds and flocks that have crossed the land, the waters, and the skies of our vast continent. We shall probe what has happened to this host of wildlife in the relatively few centuries since man arrived here, and the ways it has contributed to the civilization which now threatens it. Finally, we shall try to assess the future of wildlife in America.

Both the pronghorn antelope (right) and its close relative Stockoceras *(below and opposite) grazed New World prairies in the Ice Ages, but only the pronghorn remains. Unlike the deer's removable antlers, "prongbuck" horn cores are part of the skull. They are covered with fused hair sheaths which are shed annually. This native mammal is one of our few living links with the Pleistocene.*

Normal melt from the Big Ice filled every brook and river, created new lakes, perpetuated old marshlands. Grass grew everywhere, more grass than the new arrivals and the native herds of horses, camels, and pronghorn antelope together could eat. Trees were beyond counting, pines and cedars and hemlocks and cypress along the waterways. Farther still from the ice were maples, elms, chestnuts, sycamores, beeches, birches, and cottonwoods, with leafage, nuts, seeds, and fruits for the squirrels, mice, and rats that were native here. And for such migrants from South America as the porcupine and the armadillo.

Bison began to swarm over the vast grasslands and into the woodlands to the east. Deer were in every thicket. Moose and elk were on the flatlands and in the thin woodlands. Beavers, some as big as black bears, swarmed in the streams.

And the birds, the fish, the insects filled the land's niches. Wild geese crowded the lakes, the ponds were full of ducks, the rivers teemed with huge trout and sturgeon, the bordering oceans with cod and salmon and all the lesser fish. Whales and seals and walruses fed and migrated in the offshore waters. Whales even ran up the big rivers, up the

Hudson a hundred miles. The skies were beginning to darken with passenger pigeons.

This surely was a land of such plenty that nothing, nobody, could ever reduce it to any point of scarcity. The hunters from Asia had found a place where they could live forever. They and those who had come before them spread out over the land, from coast to coast, south all the way to Cape Horn. They became the vastly varied tribes and cultures of the American Indians.

Meanwhile, the climate was subtly changing. Whether it was a consequence of sun spots or a shift in the earth's axis, or whatever, there began, about 12,000 years ago, a gradual rise in atmospheric temperature. It rose a few degrees and the Big Ice began to melt. Slowly it melted back and floods of water poured down the rivers into the oceans. As the level of the oceans rose and the land bridge was slowly submerged again, America was cut off from Asia. This continent as we know it today was in the final stages of its formation as trees and grasses clothed the ice-scarred land, and as the dried-up coves, harbors, and islands along all our coasts gradually became once more the watery places they are now.

This did not happen overnight, but over several thousand years. And before the Big Melt had been completed, the Great Die-off began.

There are various theories about what happened and why, none of them conclusive. All we really know is that the vast herds from Asia and many animals native to America were wiped out. Was it because the climate changed? There had been climate changes before, and these were warm-blooded animals, not the cold-blooded reptiles that perished when the earth chilled off at the end of the Age of Dinosaurs. Was it because of a change of vegetation in most areas? The change was gradual, and these were more or less adaptable animals. Could intensive hunting have killed them? It seems impossible, with so few hunters and so many animals. The number of early Americans at the end of the Ice Age has been estimated at no more than one million. Perhaps one in four was a healthy male hunter, a maximum of 250,000.

And yet, man has never had to be a conservative hunter until today. The Ice Age hunter had only crude weapons, the flint-tipped spear and arrow,

the chipped stone knife. But he had methods more effective than those weapons; and the idea that the ancestral Indians took only what they needed, though a pretty myth, is only a myth. If they wanted meat they drove a herd into a bog, took enough for a few meals and left the rest to die there. We cannot be sure when the first hunters trapped animals in a ring of fire, but paleontologists have reconstructed how they drove a large herd of bison over a cliff to get a dozen skins and one big feast.

Whatever the reason, fewer and fewer long-horned bison were found, year after year, and camels and horses disappeared along with most of the musk oxen. Even the big cats, the dire wolves, and the cave bears became fewer, with the shrinking of the herds on which they preyed.

How long this took, nobody can say within a few thousand years, but in geological terms it was sudden. Whatever the cause, North American wildlife was back almost where it had been before the Ice Age, with most of the immigrants from Asia wiped out. Except for one new and vastly important species, *Homo sapiens*. It was almost as though the vanished herds had fulfilled a purpose—they had led man to America.

Exotic invaders like the porcupine shuffled up from South America after the Panama isthmus was created by volcanic action in the Tertiary Epoch 65,000,000 to 2,500,000 years ago. Later, the arctic ice cap consumed ocean waters, enabling the wolf and other Eurasian immigrants to cross the exposed seabed (below). Here to meet and compete with the newcomers were natives like the cougar.

15

Awestruck at 20,000 lesser sandhill cranes on Nebraska's Platte River en route from Mexican wintering grounds to Canadian nesting areas, photographer Ron Klataske noted how overpowering were "the roar of wings and the cries of cranes."

Today more than 50 North American species follow ancient waterfowl flyways (below). Over the millennia migration patterns have shifted and in this century numbers of birds have decreased, chiefly because man has preempted the wetlands.

To lure a tasty meal from the sky, Indians made tule rush duck decoys like those above, found in a Nevada cave.

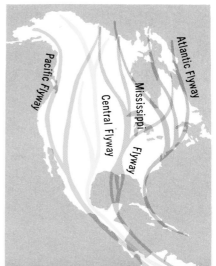

MER DES ETILLES:

TROPIQVE DE CANCER:

LA MER OCCEANE:

MER DESPAIGNE:

MER DE FRANCE:

CANADA

OCHELAGA

TERRE DES BRETONS

Assumption

ISLAND

QVE: LA TERRE DV LABOVREVR:

Splendid with stags, unicorns, and hunting dogs, this
1546 map of North America (which is more recognizable
when turned upside down) focuses on the Kingdom of
Saguenay along Canada's St. Lawrence River. French

cartographer Pierre Desceliers based it on reports from
Cartier's three voyages. The map reflects tales of rich
kingdoms told by captive Huron Indians, and the Renais-
sance concept of man in harmony with wildlife.

Meanwhile the world's other continents were accepting the presence of man—man amid the animals he worshiped, tamed, and hunted. Slowly cultures evolved and some became civilizations. Men took what they wanted from the earth around them, felled forests, fouled rivers, mined coal and stone and metals; fought among themselves for cropland, for timber, for peltry. Europe became a center of civilization, its forests largely cut, most of its native animals slain, its nearby waters largely fished out.

Europeans learned to navigate the oceans, learned the shape of Africa and Asia. Venturesome fishermen sailed westward, following schools of fish into new waters, finding rich fisheries off Newfoundland. Despite distances, despite another minor Ice Age, the Europeans pressed on over the westward horizon.

In the ways of man, such a seemingly minor matter as the flavor and preservation of food can prompt journeys to the ends of the world. Europe's monarchs, without exception, liked good food—the finest of wild boar, the fattest venison, the richest wild goose and grouse and pheasant. But without refrigeration, the royal cooks had to use herbs and spices by the handful to mask the smell and taste of meat a few days after it was butchered. Spices came from China and the Indies, by caravan much of the way, and were expensive when they could be had at all. If a wise and fortunate navigator could find a more direct route to those Oriental spice groves, a king could have spice aplenty, perhaps even his own spice plantation.

Of course there were other reasons for financing a voyage by a Columbus or a Cabot or a Cortez. Wars, large and small, had pauperized many of the royal houses, and rivalries were bitter among them. Perhaps there was gold or other treasure for the royal coffers out there in the mysterious beyond. Certainly there would be prestige and colonial power.

So Columbus made his voyage of discovery for Queen Isabella of Spain, and five years later, another Italian, Giovanni Caboto, was dispatched by England's King Henry VII to sail west and "seek out, discover and find whatsoever isles, countreys or provinces of the heathen and infidels," raise there the English "banners and ensignes," and in re-

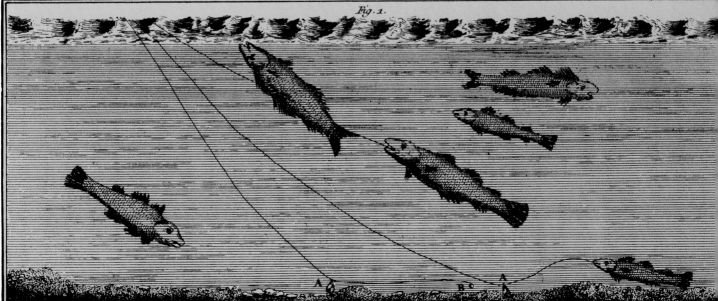

Fig. 1.

ward to have a monopoly of transatlantic trade.

Caboto—his name was anglicized and thereafter he would be known as John Cabot—and a crew of only 18 men, including his son Sebastian, headed across the North Atlantic in the little ship *Matthew* in 1497. They raised the banner of St. George somewhere on the northeast coast, probably Newfoundland, and proclaimed possession in the name of England. Sebastian Cabot's report is scanty but the only one that has survived. It is one of the first looks we have of mainland America through European eyes.

The land, he said, "is full of white bears, and stags far greater than ours. It yields plenty of fish, and those very great, as seals, and those which we commonly call salmon; there are soles also above a yard in length: but especially there is a great abundance of that kind of fish which the savages call baccalaos." The baccalaos were codfish.

The Cabot party spent about three weeks "exploring," but never went as much as five miles inland. Because Cabot brought back neither spices nor gold, the voyage was put down as a failure, though England eventually based her territorial claims in America on it.

Meanwhile, French and Portuguese fishermen began working the Grand Banks, since most of Europe was Catholic and ate enormous quantities of fish. Cod had been found easiest to cure and keep, and here were more cod than all Europe could eat. The French came ashore and set up a few places to dry and cure fish on the beach. Eventually they expanded these settlements to the St. Lawrence Gulf area and made them the basis of their claim to this New World fishing empire.

But the sixteenth century was going to be the Spanish century in America. Almost a hundred years before the English colonists arrived in Virginia the Spanish adventurers had been over the land from Florida to Texas and from Texas to

The parka-clad Newfoundland fisherman in the 1715 drawing (opposite) was a key figure in a European industry that had been bringing the Old and New Worlds together for 200 years. Cod liver oil and salted fish were the rewards. Other early prints show the strong hooks and "grounde lynes" used to land the 60-pound cod.

California. They had wallowed through the muckland and swamps of Florida and piney uplands of Georgia looking only for gold or gems comparable to the treasure Cortez had found among the Aztecs in Mexico, Pizzaro had taken from the Incas in Peru, and Quesada had plundered from the Chibcha in Colombia. They had seen the moss-festooned live oaks, eerie in shadows even in daylight, like a scene from another planet in the moonlight. They undoubtedly saw alligators, though their reports do not mention them. We wait for William Bartram to describe this "subtle, greedy" but "prodigious" animal two centuries later:

"The alligator when full grown is a very large and terrible creature, and of prodigious strength, activity and swiftness in the water. I have seen them twenty feet in length, and some are supposed to be twenty-two or twenty-three feet. Their body is as large as that of a horse, their shape exactly resembles that of a lizard, except their tail, which is flat or cuneiform, being compressed on each side and gradually diminishing from the abdomen to the extremity, which, with the whole body, is covered with horny plates or squammae, impenetrable when on the body of the live animal, even to a rifle ball, except about their head and just behind their forelegs or arms, where it is said they are only vulnerable. The head of a full grown one is about three feet, and the mouth opens nearly the same length; their eyes are small in proportion and seem sunk deep in the head, by means of the prominency of the brows; the nostrils are large, inflated and prominent on the top . . . Only the upper jaw moves, which they raise almost perpendicular, so as to form a right angle with the lower one . . . When they clap their jaws together it causes a surprising noise, like that which is made by forcing a heavy plank with violence upon the ground, and may be heard at a great distance . . . But what is most surprising to a stranger is the incredible loud and terrifying roar which they are capable of making, especially in the spring season, their breeding time. It most resembles very distant thunder, not only shaking the air and waters, but causing the earth to tremble."

Somehow those Spanish conquistadores wandered all over Florida and the Gulf Coast without leaving us a record of such creatures.

From 1528 to 1531 a company of 80 Spaniards exploring the Gulf Coast from Tampa Bay north and west was reduced by wilderness perils to three men who with their surviving leader, Cabeza de Vaca, reached Mexico City. They were the first

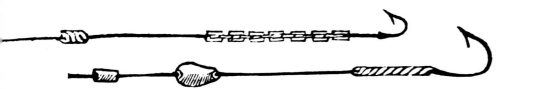

21

Europeans to see—at least to report seeing—American bison (not the Asian immigrant but the American native). "Hunch-backed cows," Cabeza de Vaca described them. "They have small horns like the cows of Morocco; their hair is very long and wooly like a rug. Some are tawny, others black." And he said their flesh was "finer and fatter" than that of the Spanish beef cattle.

As late as the eighteenth century bison in considerable numbers roamed the South and the East excepting the coastal areas of New England. In 1693 they were being killed for meat by French hunters at Pensacola, and six years later they were reported by the French near the present site of Biloxi.

In 1539 Hernando de Soto set out for Florida with a big new expedition, 600 men, 200-odd horses, a pack of fighting dogs to kill or harass Indians, and a herd of 13 swine. The swine were to provide meat, which seems strange in an area abounding in deer. But those Spaniards seemed to think of the wilderness as either devoid of edible life or somehow untrustworthy, maybe even poisonous. Yet there was no mention of anyone in de Soto's party being bitten by the poisonous snakes so common in the swamps and sandy uplands and in the palmetto barrens. It is possible that the herd of swine took care of the snakes. Even domestic swine seem to have a tolerance for snake venom and kill and eat reptiles when they get a chance. De Soto's hogs throve, whatever their diet, and multiplied until there was a herd of 700.

The de Soto expedition was prowling through the South—perhaps storming would be a better word for a party that size—four years, north as far as Arkansas, down the Mississippi to the Gulf, and on to Mexico. De Soto died along the way. The pigs that escaped and those stolen by the Indians undoubtedly became the breeding stock for the vicious wild hogs that still live in the Okefenokee Swamp. They were not, however, in any way related to the peccaries or javelinas of southwest Texas and southern Arizona and New Mexico. The peccary is our one native pig-like animal.

The de Soto expedition was probably the most spectacular of the Spanish failures, but it was the most extensive exploration of North America yet undertaken except that by Coronado.

A Spanish provincial governor, Coronado had heard exciting tales from Cabeza de Vaca about the gold-rich Seven Cities of Cibola. He set out in January, 1540 with about 300 Spanish soldiers from Mexico, "a large number" of slaves, 1,000 horses, several hundred pack animals, and a herd of cattle and sheep to provide meat. They went north through the San Pedro Valley, then up the Gila River to the Pueblo country of Arizona. They discovered the Grand Canyon and Indians living in multi-storied pueblos, but found no treasure. They saw Rocky Mountain "goats," and "gray lions and leopards," probably cougars and wildcats. As the expedition headed north from New Mexico, the travelers certainly saw jaguars. The jaguar, also called *el tigre*, is the biggest cat in America. In those days the jaguar was native to the area as far north as the Red River in Arkansas. Some debatable records say its explosive, snarling roar was known and feared as far east as the Carolinas. Because early Spaniards placed a bounty on it, the jaguar was almost wiped out by the 1800s. One was reported in New Mexico in 1903, and an occasional animal still wanders across the border, but the species is all but gone from the States.

The Coronado party turned east through New Mexico and met a nomad party of Plains Indians, probably Apaches. Having no horses, the Indians used dogs for pack animals and to draw small travois. Still traveling east, the expedition found Indian villages with flocks of tamed turkeys which Coronado's men called "chickens." Quite a number of pueblos also raised turkeys. The people of the Southwest, the sedentary tribes, kept the turkeys to have not only the meat but also the feathers, which they used in ceremonials and even in making feather robes. These were fashioned of cotton yarn with downy feathers woven in by their shafts for extra warmth and beauty.

The expedition turned north again and went all the way to Kansas. After traveling 2,500 miles, Coronado returned to Mexico and received a cold welcome from the viceroy because he had found no gleaming cities and brought back no gold. But the Southwest had been explored, in a way. The Spanish knew something of its extent, its vast leagues of grass, its millions of bison, its lesser herds of pronghorns. Coronado had seen the plains grizzlies, the "great white bears" that followed the bison

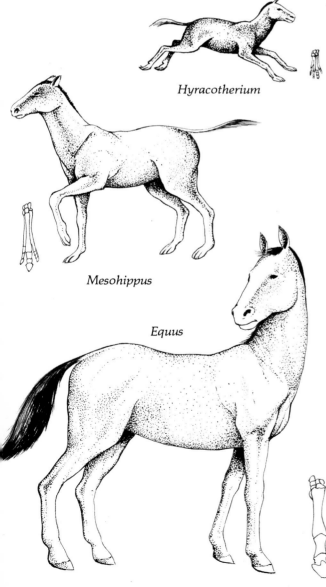

Hyracotherium

Mesohippus

Equus

herds, and had pronounced them terrible and most dangerous. But a full description of the grizzlies would have to wait almost 250 years for Meriwether Lewis.

Coronado saw and no doubt had his troubles with prairie dogs, which at that time the Spanish called "barking squirrels." Their burrows are dangerous to horses and cattle unfamiliar with the area. An animal may step into one of the holes and break a leg, especially if it is running. Undoubtedly some of Coronado's mounts or pack animals were lost in just this way.

The old tales that say the Indians first got horses by stealing them from the Coronado expedition seem to be pure fancy. The Indians he met were afraid of the horses, sometimes more than of the men. But the expedition no doubt left strays, both of horses and mules or burros, that went wild and eventually they or their offspring were captured by the Indians.

In 1513 Vasco Nunez de Balboa crossed the Isthmus of Panama and laid claim to the Pacific Ocean and all shores it washed upon. In 1542 Juan Rodriguez Cabrillo, another Spanish gold seeker, sailed north from Mexico up the coast of California as far as Oregon. He saw majestic forests of Douglas fir and some of the gigantic redwoods. He saw the almost incredible richness of those shores and their quiet ocean. The seals and sea lions on the rocky islets just offshore made a constant uproar with their barking. Gulls screamed overhead. Near the kelp beds the dark, sleek sea otters dived for abalones and lay on their backs in the gently rocking water while they opened the shells and ate the meat of those succulent shellfish. Elephant seals, some of them fifteen feet long, all of them hog-fat with the oily blubber that would lead to their destruction

Fleet native of North America, the horse evolved over a period of 50,000,000 years. Tiny Hyracotherium *was the earliest, running on the balls of its feet (upper left drawing). Then, by natural selection,* Mesohippus *shed the foot's lesser bones (center); ultimately Pleistocene* Equus *ran on its middle toe, the firm hoof of today's horse (bottom). Despite its speed, the horse became extinct here, reappearing only when Spanish invaders rode into battle (top). Later, rounding up strays from the early Spanish missions, Indians made the horse American once again.*

23

by the nineteenth century whalers, played like porpoises in the rolling water, and awkwardly hauled themselves up on the beaches of the islands of Santa Barbara. But Cabrillo saw no rich cities, and the nuggets in the Sacramento Valley would not be discovered for another three centuries.

As a capstone to their splendid century, the Spanish established a colony on the continent's east coast in 1565. They built a fort of coquina shell rock on the Florida coast and named it St. Augustine. Sir Francis Drake sacked and burned St. Augustine in 1586, but the Spanish soon restored it. It was the first permanent European settlement in what would become the continental United States.

Nonetheless, the Spanish regarded their North American conquests as fruitless. And the supreme irony is that, treasure-oriented as they were, they gained no conception of the real wealth of this continent. That remained to be discovered and exploited by the English, the French, and the Dutch.

The Cabots had made their voyages and claimed the whole Northeast for England at the end of the fifteenth century. Subsequent British explorers and settlers would have welcomed gold, if they had found any; but eventually they saw that America's wealth lay in its fisheries, its wildlife, its forests, and its soil. Its fisheries—both freshwater and salt—were unparalleled. American cod, dried or salted, was already in great demand throughout Europe. England also needed wood for shipbuilding, for charcoal, for wood-ash. The charcoal was essential for making glass and steel. The wood-ash lye was needed to make soap for the weavers of woolen cloth. And England's forests had been largely cut. America's forests seemed endless, from the very seacoast as far inland as anyone had yet ventured. Her soil was so rich that the Indians, even with indifferent farming methods, grew more maize, beans, and squash than they could eat. An English farmer could grow tremendous crops in such soil.

In 1585 Sir Walter Raleigh's Roanoke adventure began on a sandy island off the North Carolina coast. That adventure ended with the disappearance of all the colonists and the labeling of the episode as "The Lost Colony." Thereafter the English were laggard in establishing settlements. They would need another generation before becoming the continent's great colonizers.

The French were more opportunistic than the Spanish or the English. In 1534 Jacques Cartier discovered the St. Lawrence River and ascended it as far as the site of Montreal. In addition to claiming all that area for France, his voyage had a number of noteworthy incidents. One of the first was the incredible number of birds Cartier saw. On the first rocky island, still well out to sea, were so many birds that "all the ships of France might load a cargo of them without perceiving that any had been removed." On the island now known as Funk Island were thousands of "queer, large, black and white fowl, obviously and appetizingly edible, as big as geese and so fat that it is marvelous." They were unable to fly, for they had "only small wings about the size of a man's hand." They were great auks, and within half an hour Cartier's men had clubbed enough of them to fill two longboats. The expedition feasted on the fresh poultry and salted down four or five casks of them for each ship.

They also saw a young polar bear and butchered it. "His flesh," Cartier wrote in his report, "was as good to eat as that of a two-year-old heifer." But the flightless auks were the particular treasure for the sailors, as they were for virtually all others who came near Funk Island in the next century or so. Two years after Cartier's first visit an Englishman named Robert Hore stopped at Funk and spread a canvas sail from shore to ship, then had his men march a holdful of auks from their rocky haven to a butcher shop aboard ship. Auks at that time nested as far south as Maine and there was a winter population of them in Massachusetts Bay. But the southern colonies were soon destroyed. Their eggs as well as their flesh were good

The frog was revered by desert Indians as an animal spirit which led them to water; hence its shape traced on a bowl (above) by a Hohokam hand. Coronado may have seen the ruins (opposite) of the artist's ancestral home.

to eat, and they furnished down and feathers as well as oil and even codfish bait. They hadn't a chance. In 1785 George Cartwright wrote that "several crews of men . . . live all summer on that island (Funk) for the sole purpose of killing birds for the sake of their feathers, the destruction which they have made is incredible. If a stop is not soon put to that practice, the whole breed will be diminished to almost nothing." He does not mention that the birds' carcasses were also boiled down for their oil. (The last great auk was killed in June, 1844 on Eldey Island off the coast of Iceland, by fishermen collecting bird specimens for an Icelandic bird collector.)

In the St. Lawrence Gulf Cartier found another island, now called Greenly, covered with red-beaked puffins, or sea parrots. Expert swimmers and divers, they came to land mainly for breeding season, in June and July. They crowded the island so closely that their burrows were like the cells in a honeycomb. Nearby was an island covered with the down-lined nests of eider ducks and "eggs in great quantity," which the seamen gathered and ate. And still another island was covered with the seaweed nests of gannets, big white birds with black-tipped wings, three feet long and with a four-foot wingspread. A Jesuit priest with Cartier's company said, "Everywhere may be seen geese, ducks, herons, cranes, swans, coots, and other birds whose habit it is to seek their living from the waves."

As they went on up the St. Lawrence they saw walruses, which they called "Sea Oxen," and rich areas "covered with fine trees and meadows, fields of wild oats and of pease in flower, as thick and fine as ever I saw in Brittany." There also were wild roses, strawberries, chokecherries, "parsley and other strong-smelling herbs." Cartier was greatly impressed by the trees—cedar, yew, pine, elm, ash, willow—and wild pigeons "fluttering in their branches." This may have been one of the first mentions of the passenger pigeons.

Soon after this he returned to France. In May of 1535, Cartier came back to the St. Lawrence. Again he stopped at Funk Island and stocked up with great auks, which the French now called penguins.

The real founder of New France in America was Samuel de Champlain. He came to the St. Lawrence in 1604 and established a colony and trading post at Quebec in 1608. He wasn't looking for gold or gems or magic elixir or anything except practical trade in American peltry, which by then was commanding a good price in Europe. The trading post bought beaver skins from the Indians, and mink and marten and fisher, and buckskins when they were offered.

Champlain went up the St. Lawrence, as Cartier had. He explored the New England coast, then worked inland and explored upper New York where he discovered the lake that bears his name, and went on to the Great Lakes. He made friends with the Huron and Algonkian Indians, enemies of the Iroquois, thus setting up an alliance and a hostility that eventually would shape American history.

He saw that upper New York had many beaver, and evidently there were even more to the west and to the north of the Great Lakes. The Indians talked as though beaver were as many as the birds. He saw deer, and he saw elk and moose, even more of them than deer. In the lakes, including Lake Champlain, he found huge lake trout, four and five feet long, even bigger white fish, and sturgeon big enough to capsize a canoe. He also found how severe a plague of mosquitoes could be. In one report he said, "it was wonderful how cruelly they persecuted us." Others have used much stronger words to describe the attacks of black flies, gnats, and all flying, biting insects that were lumped under the name, "mosquitoes."

Champlain made a succession of trips to the St. Lawrence and the Great Lakes. He probably learned more about the country than any European except the Spaniards in the Southwest. It was largely through his efforts that French claims to Canada were maintained.

The die had been cast. Not by the Spanish or the English, but by the French, by the men who saw the significance of all those beaver in the American streams, all that peltry in Indian hands.

The meat animals had led ancient man across the land bridge from Siberia to Alaska. The fish had led modern man across the forbidding North Atlantic to the northeast coast of America. Now the beaver would lead men inland, to discover the rest of this continent's incredible wealth—eventually, even its gold.

Paul Kane's Salish dancers display raven masks, and a blanket woven from mountain goat wool in "Medicine Mask Dance."

EAST INTO A
WILD EDEN

*From Asia came the first Americans, peopling a virgin realm and honoring its
animals in tribal rites like the Salish Medicine Mask Dance. Indian artifacts reflecting
dependence on animals have been found along the legendary trail of the Lenni
Lenape tribe who crossed the continent about 336 to 1498 A.D.*

Soapstone hunter and bear with ivory knife and teeth. Opposite: left to right, incised ivory needle case with fish effigy stoppers, sea lion amulet carved from a bear's tooth.

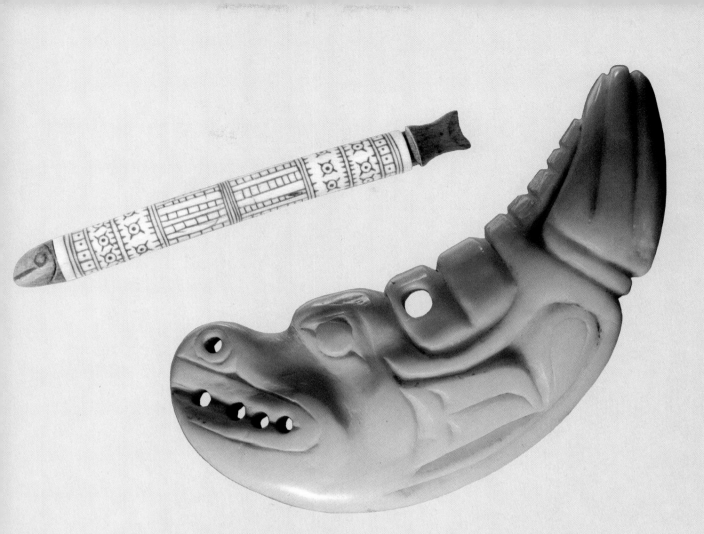

"IT WOULD BE GOOD TO LIVE ON THE OTHER SIDE"

Thus did a Lenni Lenape Indian legend, entitled the Wallamolum, explain their ancestors' decision to cross the Bering Strait. Ultimately they reached the Atlantic—where they were called Delaware Indians. Their story was preserved in verse and in pictograph (below) painted on sticks. Though the sticks vanished, the tale they tell survives in an 1833 study by naturalist Constantine Rafinesque. Unsung then, his findings gain credibility as research confirms the legend of migrants traversing an already inhabited continent. In Alaska the Lenni Lenape would have met the Eskimo, a hunter who could slay a bear and carve from its fang an amulet for sea lion hunts; a fisherman who shaped his wood-and-ivory needle case in a fish's image; an artist who might spend days of arctic dark etching in stone and ivory a moment of triumph in his lifelong duel with a harsh environment.

Head Beaver and Big Bird said to one another, "Let us all go to Snake Island." (Book III, verse 14)

". . . the Northerners were of one mind and the Easterners were of one mind: it would be good to live on the other side of the frozen water." (III, 16)

"Things turned out well for all those who had stayed at the shore of water frozen hard as rocks, and for those at the great hollow well." (III, 17)

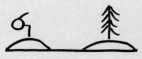

". . . all came from Snow Mountain and the forest country; the West Delaware came out of humor, for they preferred the old Turtle land." (III, 20)

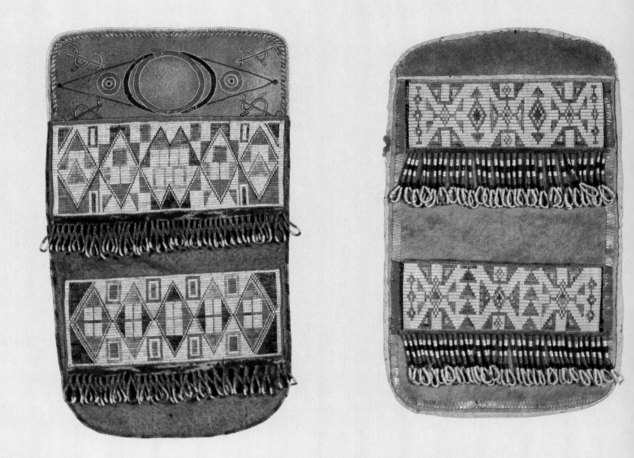

"A VAST COUNTRY, A GOOD LAND"

Probing a continent more vast than they knew, the wanderers entered the "land of little sticks" where conifers mark the tundra's edge. Remaining on the Alaska plateau but briefly, they explored the Yukon Valley and moved to warmer lands southward. Today the plateau is occupied by Athapaskan tribes who established a foothold there in relatively recent times. Those pioneering forefathers found how to survive on fish, birds, and berries while watching always for the caribou. Its meat warmed their bellies (unlike Eskimos, Athapaskans cooked their meals), and its bone made a varied kit of tools. Its skin, adorned with porcupine quills, made handsome bags for their belongings. Scraped, rubbed soft, sewn with sinew into a coat with the hair side in, then painted at the wearer's whim, caribou hide warmed an Indian's back and retained its soft hues years later.

"Long ago people like the Delaware were in a forest by a lake." (Book IV, verse 1)

"Bald Eagle was the one traveling along a road, and all those others, too . . ." (IV, 2)

". . . towards Snake Island, a vast country, a good land, where cold winds never blow." (IV, 3)

"After Fine Old Head, White Owl was chief at the forest land." (IV, 8)

Caribou-hide coat with painted design. Opposite: buckskin bags decorated with dyed and woven porcupine quills.

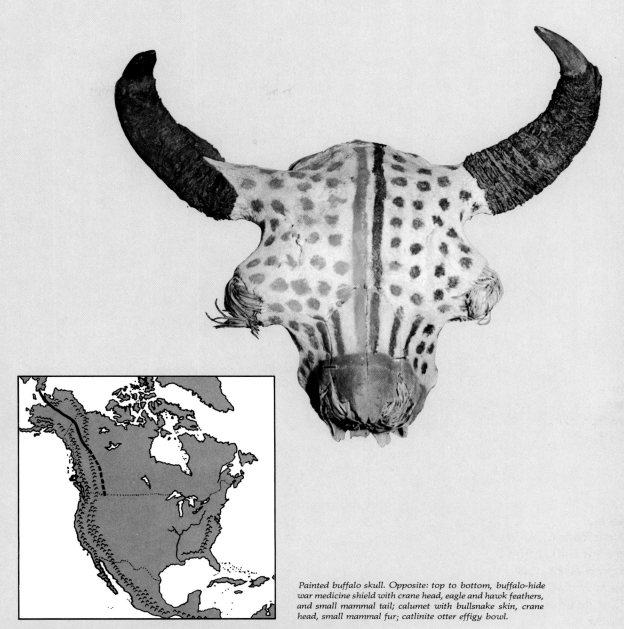

Painted buffalo skull. Opposite: top to bottom, buffalo-hide war medicine shield with crane head, eagle and hawk feathers, and small mammal tail; calumet with bullsnake skin, crane head, small mammal fur; catlinite otter effigy bowl.

"HE CALLED FOR AN EMIGRATION TOWARD THE EAST"

A new generation looked east from "Snow Mountain"—probably the Rockies around 800 A.D.—to a land of arrow-straight horizons: the Great Plains. Later, tribes like the Crow, Sioux, and Arapaho drew mighty medicine from the spirits of plains animals. A Crow shield of buffalo hide, rolled on the ground, foretold a venture's success if it fell face up. A pipe of snakeskin and birds' heads, with an otter effigy bowl, protected its Sioux owner. And a buffalo skull housed the "Above One" during the Sun Dance of the Arapaho.

"Next in order was handsome One Feather, engrossed in hate, who wanted to go away . . ." (Book IV, verse 31)

". . . because he was angry; he called for an emigration toward the east, but some went off secretly." (IV, 32)

"Those at Snow Mountain were happy, and made One Who Is Beloved chief." (IV, 33)

"Once again they were in a settlement by the Yellow River, where berries were abundant among the rocks and stones." (IV, 34)

"LET THOSE GOING EAST BE MANY"

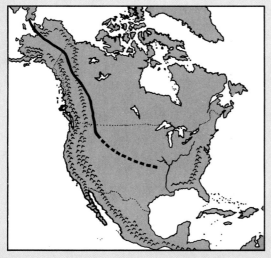

Most of the Lenni Lenape clans journeyed eastward through the plains. Then the horse was unknown; the Plains Indian hunted the buffalo on foot. He had seen the great beasts ignore the passing wolf, so he wrapped himself in wolfskin and crawled on hands and knees to within an arrow's flight. When the herd ambled off to wintering grounds, he had to turn to other fare. At winter's end he probably resorted to ritual prayers to bring the shaggy grazers back. So did his distant descendants; painter George Catlin captured their Buffalo Dance in the mid-1800s. By then horses had made Indians mobile, dependent on the herds they followed. So they mounted a buffalo effigy on a ritual shield, while a buffalo hide sounded the hollow heartbeat of a three-legged drum. In ceremony as in life, the Plains Indian and the buffalo had become inseparable.

"Now when daylight came, he spoke three times: "Let those going east be many." (Book IV, verse 48)

"They separated at [Fish, or Mississippi] River; and the ones who were lazy returned to Snow Mountain." (IV, 49)

"When Lean-to Man was chief, the Tallegewi were in possession of the east." (IV, 50)

"When Strong Friend was chief, he wanted to go to the Eastern country." (IV, 51)

Clockwise, rawhide-covered drum, beaded buckskin arm bands with porcupine quill and feather danglers, and rawhide dance shield with painted buffalo design. Opposite: painting of Indian dancers wearing buffalo-head masks by George Catlin.

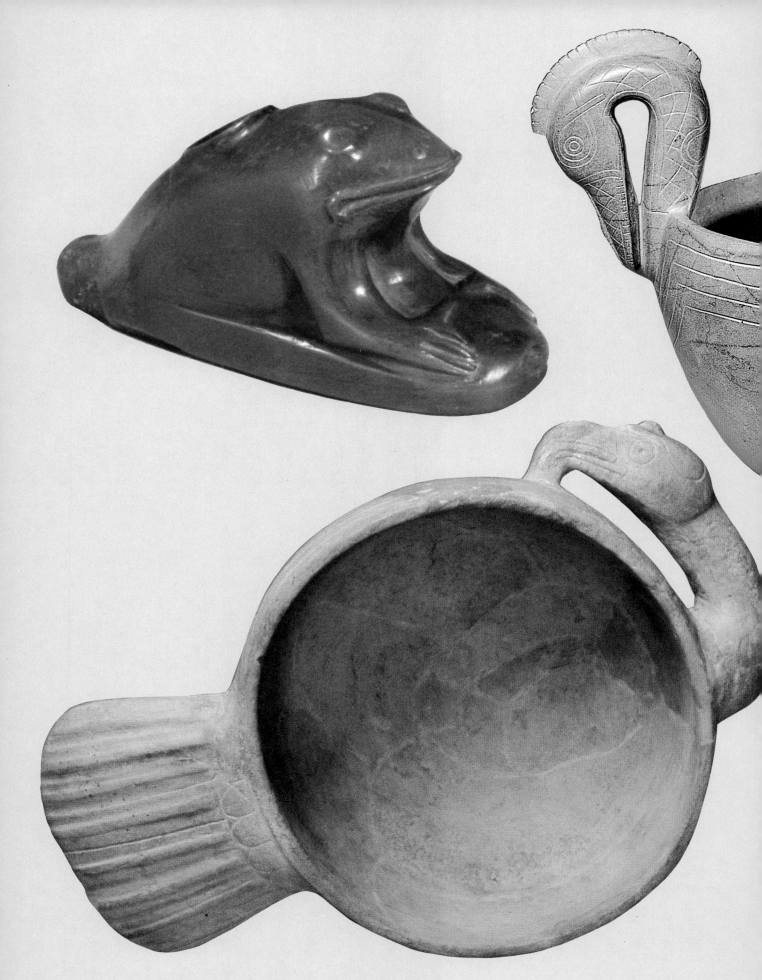

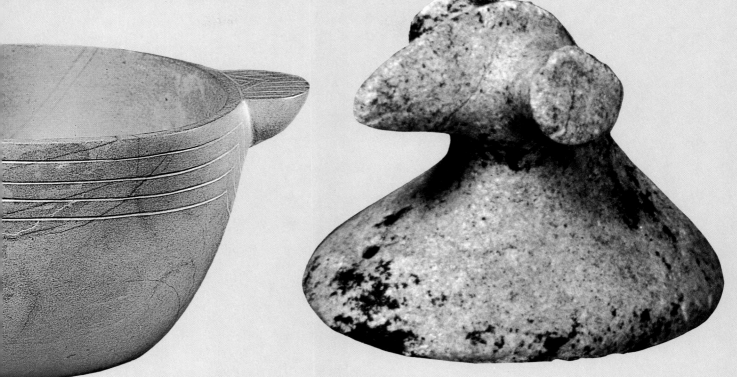

Carved pop-eyed birdstone. Opposite: clockwise, frog effigy pipe, wood-duck effigy bowl of diorite, and turkey effigy bowl of limestone.

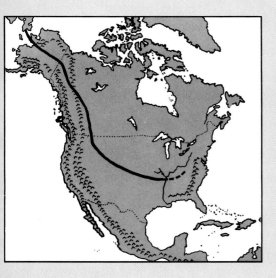

"MUCH FARMING . . . MANY BERRIES . . . MANY RIVERS"

At last the sojourners entered Eden—the Eastern woodlands. Nuts and berries ripened on tree and bush; deer, ducks, and turkeys fattened in forest, bog, and meadow. Indians for millennia had sunk roots here, adding to nature's gifts the products of farming. Left with leisure, they developed complex cultures that reared earthen mounds for tombs and temples. Most mounds had been abandoned when Lenni Lenape tribesmen arrived. But inside them a frog stood guard on a ceremonial stone pipe, a crested wood duck and a fan-tailed turkey kept vigil from stone bowls, a pop-eyed birdstone atlatl weight boded well for the hunt —each a tribute to the artist and to the culture that could afford such specialists. Not all was idyll; even the bounty of soil and game could be depleted in time. Then the tribe would again trek the trails or paddle "on many rivers" to better lands.

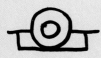
"Long ago, all kept peace with each other there in the Talega country." (Book V, verse 1)

"When White Wildcat was chief, there was much farming." (V, 3)

"When Old Bird was chief, there were many berries." (V, 6)

"When One Who Paddles was chief, they travelled on many rivers." (V, 8)

"THEY WERE AT THE MIGHTY WATER"

Journey's end; the wanderers had reached the sea. Here, too, men puffed stone pipes in the image of animals like the squirrel. The sea added wampum, purple-and-white beads made from quahog clam shell. Now came Europeans "floating in from the east," their tall ships and Christian cross symbolized in the Wallamolum's 163rd verse. Soon the white man would name these Indians Delawares. He would treaty with them, as did William Penn in 1683. They gave Penn the wampum belt shown above, inspiring Edward Hicks 150 years later to include the scene in one of his many idealized paintings of "The Peaceable Kingdom." By then the Delawares knew few white friends as they suffered forced marches to reservations in the West. "The Wallamolum was written . . . to record our glory," mourns a 19th-century Delaware scribe. "Shall I write another to record our fall?"

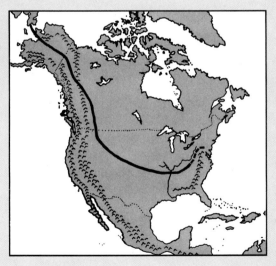

"When One Who Looks On was chief, they went to the Talega Mountains." (Book V, verse 19)

"When One Who Becomes Fat was chief, they were in the sassafras country." (V, 25)

"When Red-Paint Soul was chief, they were at the mighty water." (V, 28)

"When One Who Takes Things By Accident was chief, there came from yonder persons floating in from the east; the Whites were coming." (V, 39-40)

Wampum belt of clam-shell beads; below, Edward Hicks' painting, "The Peaceable Kingdom." Opposite: squirrel effigy pipe of steatite.

Taming the Forest Wilderness

There were six-foot sturgeon in the James River. The marshes were alive with ducks and geese, all manner of waterfowl. There were deer and wild turkeys and grouse in the woods. Yet the colony of hungry people set down in the midst of this natural plenty were afraid or unable to take and use it. All of the Jamestown colonists sent over by the South Virginia Company of London, in the early spring of 1607, might have starved if their leader, John Smith, had not bartered with Indians for food. Even with that help, less than one half survived the first year.

They were a sorry crew—misfits, quarrelsome, unprepared in just about every way to wrest a living from the wilderness. The settlement survived its first few years only because Captain Smith was a tough, determined man. Eventually they learned to grow their own corn and vegetables, and to hunt and fish for the plenty at their doorstep. But not soon enough. By 1610 scarcely 60 of the first 600 arrivals were still alive.

Much of the suffering has been traced to yellow fever and brackish drinking water, yet we are haunted by the question of why they hungered in the midst of plenty. Was it fear of the dark, surrounding Virginia forest which kept them from going on hunting trips as the Indians did? Or was it distrust of the savages themselves which kept the starving colonists close to the palisaded huts of Jamestown?

And why did John Smith and his successors make frequent voyages to New England for winter supplies of fish? We know they netted sturgeon on its spring run up the James, and John Smith later wrote "in the small rivers all the year there is good plenty of small fish, so that with hooks those that would take pains had sufficient." A net stretched across any small creek in tidewater would fill with striped bass, northern croakers, spots, sea trout, whiting, chubb, or shad—whatever was running at the time. Did the settlers run out of hemp for making nets? Or did they no longer have the strength?

Answers to the Jamestown enigma elude us, but the Virginia colonists' bitter experience posed questions which each succeeding wave of settlers would have to answer in its own way. Questions about the skills, the human qualities, and the supplies needed to conquer the wilderness by turning its

This delicate 1588 map recalls Sir Francis Drake's 1586 sacking of Santo Domingo for gold and to replenish stores. His sailors ate the turtle and alligator depicted here, but his artist's other sea creatures are pure fancy.

Indians and colonists depended on white-tailed deer for more than venison. They made soap and candles of its tallow, stuffed saddles and chairs with its hair, cut thongs and garments from its hide. The buckskin cloak embellished with tiny shells below belonged to Chief Powhatan. New York Indian agent Col. Guy Johnson (right) sports buckskin leggings in an eighteenth century portrait.

Antlers too were used, for handles and trim. They develop from nubs of soft, sensitive tissue in May to branching clubs in June; October brings a rubbing-off of velvet, exposing bonehard antler. Finally antlers are shed, yielding calcium to gnawing rodents.

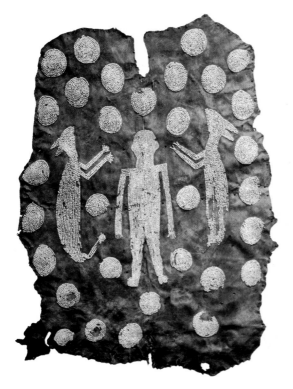

cycles of abundance and scarcity into food, shelter, warmth, and clothing. The raw wilderness would be their teacher and, on its own terms, would forge a new people.

In the end it was a New World plant, tobacco, which brought these necessities to the long-suffering Virginia colonists and which made Jamestown England's first permanent settlement in America. Some tobacco plants introduced by John Rolfe from the West Indies and Venezuela, crossed with native Virginia strains, commanded six times the price of wheat on the London market. They also shipped potash, pitch, sassafras, sturgeon, and caviar. By 1616 the colony had begun to prosper. In 1620 more than a thousand new settlers came over to seek their fortunes.

In 1620 a group of 100 religious dissenters, planning to settle near Jamestown, was blown off course and landed instead in Massachusetts Bay. The Pilgrims, as they called themselves, became the Plymouth Colony. Luckily, they were befriended by an Indian chief Samoset who taught them to catch fish with weirs, to plant fish as fertilizer with maize, and to snare deer. Although only 50 of the company, half of them children, survived the difficult first year, the colonists apparently benefited from the lessons of Jamestown. By the autumn of 1621 they not only harvested a good crop, they shot a few deer and migrant ducks, they dried berries, and made wine from wild grapes.

In October that year William Bradford, the colony's leader, invited friendly Indians to join the colonists in a three-day feast of thanksgiving. Massasoit, another Indian chief, came with 90 warriors. When they saw how little food the colonists had for such a gathering the Indians went out and killed enough deer to feed everyone. Tradition says they feasted on venison, ducks, geese, and turkey, and on pumpkins and Indian corn.

Still that Massachusetts Bay area was not exactly an Eden. A New England November can be, as some said, "cold and despairing." As Bradford put it, "What could they see but a hideous and desolate wilderness full of wild beasts and wild men?" Oliver Cromwell, hearing and reading the settlers' descriptions, called New England "that desert and barren wilderness."

Others, approaching in spring or summer, got a different impression. When Raleigh brought his first ill-fated colonists to this country, he reported that while still off the coast they "felt a most dilicate sweete smell, though they saw no land, which ere long they espied." One of his voyagers said it was "so strong a smel, as if we had bene in the midst of some delicate garden abounding in all kind of odoriferous flowers."

The first visitors to Martha's Vineyard and Cape Cod had seen "penguins"—great auks—as well as deer, ducks, geese, and other waterfowl in amazing plenty, and a "great store of Pease, which grow in certeine plots all the Island over." And strawberries. Of all the wild plants, strawberries got the most attention. The first Europeans to reach Maine spoke of them: They were "as sweet and much bigger than ours in England."

An incredible wealth of fish and shellfish awaited the Europeans. Just offshore there were whales, and codfish five feet long. One ship's captain said that at Cape Cod his men "tooke great stor of cod fyshes the bigeste & largest I ever Saw or any man in our Ship." One traveler heard of 25-pound lobsters at Plymouth and saw several 16-pounders. One boat's crew took 50 lobsters in an hour in water only three feet deep, using only a pole with a hook fastened to it. Equally numerous and tasty were "divers sorte of shell-fish, as scallops, muscles, cockles, lobsters, crabs, oyster, and welks, exceeding good and very great."

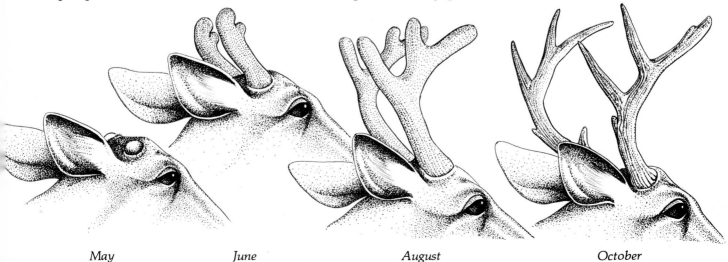

| May | June | August | October |

A feast held after the 1621 fall harvest has become a cherished legacy of our nation's origins. Only the turkey survives on our Thanksgiving menu, but wildlife on the Pilgrim board included fish, waterfowl, and venison.

Jenny Brownscombe in her latter-day painting put western-style bonnets on the eastern Indians and showed a log cabin where Plymouth had none. But she correctly depicted a society thankful for nature's bounty.

Yet even along a coast of such natural abundance, an earlier attempt at settlement had failed because of its choice of landing site. The only group of colonists sent out by the North Virginia Company of Plymouth came ashore in August of 1607 on Maine's rocky Monhegan Island. It had little to offer except fish, and the Maine winter that followed was long and bitter. The colony was disbanded the next summer. Eventually, however, the fisheries there became the largest center of English fishing on the American coast, excepting only Newfoundland. And partly through the colonists' experience there New England became the maritime center of the New World.

These early colonists clung to the coast, hacking out little clearings or enlarging those the Indians had made. Only one explorer, a Florentine, Giovanni da Verrazano, sent out by Francis I of France in 1524, had had any look at what lay a few leagues inland. Poking into a good many of the coves and inlets along the Atlantic coast, Verrazano reported "stags, deer and hares" as well as "various numbers of birds" along the New England shores. Stags probably were elk, which then were common in that area. Apparently he did not see the woods bison, which were sighted there later.

Verrazano was also the first to go inland far enough to discover that the "unbroken woodland" was actually broken in many places with clearings, some natural, some made by the Indians for farmland or to create openings where deer and other browsers could feed. He also found "wild roses, violets and many sorts of herbs and fragrant flowers different from ours."

While the English were learning to fend for themselves at Jamestown and Plymouth, the Dutch began to settle in New York harbor. In 1609 Henry Hudson, an English navigator working for the Dutch, had come down the coast, and into the mouth of the river that was to bear his name. He found Long Island and the Jersey shore to be covered with trees, most of them "the finest oaks for height and thickness that one could ever see," as well as "poplars, hickories, and plum trees that in September were blue with fruit." There were also many fine valleys where "there is good grass" and forests of elm, oak, cedar, maple, sassafras, birch, beech, and chestnut "which yield store of Mast for Swine."

Manhattan Island was "a very good woodland" with sweet water and deer. The surrounding waters were full of fish—salmon, sturgeon, shad, mullet—and oysters eight or ten inches long and three or four inches across. One oyster made "several mouthfuls." Lobsters too were plentiful in New York harbor. In fact, they were still being caught there until just before the Revolution.

Staten Island, well wooded and well watered, had wild turkeys, geese, snipe, wood hens (probably ruffed grouse), as well as deer in herds of 25 or 30. The New Jersey swamps were lined with willows and had clouds of ducks and geese. New Jersey turkeys were reported to weigh 35 to 40 pounds. Deer and black bears were common there and in Connecticut. An occasional moose or elk was seen there, too.

Hudson made his way slowly up the river, looking for a Northwest Passage to the Indies, and when he saw whales in the river as far north as present Albany, he believed he had found it. Then he came to the rapids and had to give up. It was a river, after all. But by parleying with the Indians, he had discovered some of the best fur country in the East. Nothing came of it, however, until 1621, when the Dutch West India Company was founded and established trading posts to deal in furs at Albany and on Manhattan Island. By 1626 the post on Manhattan shipped out, on one ship alone, 7,246 beaver skins, 675 otter skins, and lesser numbers of mink, wildcat, and muskrat pelts.

By the end of the century nearly all of the east coast of North America, at least from the mouth of the St. Lawrence to Florida, had a fringe of settlements, most of them English. Continuing religious dissent and innovation in England had brought the Catholics to Maryland in 1634 and the Quakers to Penn's Woodland (Pennsylvania) in 1682. Nowhere except along the big rivers, however, did settlement reach more than 50 miles inland. There was enough farming to make the colonies almost self-sustaining. Most of them were shipping grain and raw materials, timber, sassafras bark and roots, a limited amount of peltry, back to the homeland. The total population of the English colonies, not including any Caribbean outposts, was more than

250,000. No doubt about it, the English had a foothold. But only along the coast.

Meanwhile, the French had not been idle. Their main purpose was to promote the fur trade in the St. Lawrence and Ottawa valleys, and they had trading posts in Nova Scotia and along the St. Lawrence. Permanent settlement was slow, but the young French or half-breed traders and trappers, known as the *coureurs de bois*, had traveled with the Indians in their long, low canoes the length of the Great Lakes and probably as far as the Wisconsin River. The first "official" trip beyond that point was made by Louis Jolliet in 1672. Jolliet was a Frenchman born near Quebec. As usual in French or Spanish exploration, a priest was sent along; in this case it was Father Jacques Marquette. The expedition started from Mackinac Island in two canoes and followed the Indian route from Green Bay up the Fox River, over the low watershed, and down the Wisconsin into the Mississippi. On the upper reaches of the Wisconsin they found open prairies, hills, and woodland where there was practically no small game, but "deer and moose in considerable numbers."

About 100 miles down the Wisconsin, Jolliet and Marquette reached the upper Mississippi, at that point a relatively small river. As they went down the stream, the wooded shoreline changed to rich prairies with scattered trees. There were deer and moose along the banks, but no bison. Also birds they called "bustards," probably wild geese.

The Jolliet party had taken no fish on the Wisconsin, but on the Mississippi there were "monstrous fish" that could not be ignored. One, according to Marquette, "struck so violently against our canoes that I took it for a large tree about to knock us to pieces." It probably was a huge Mississippi catfish, but it could have been a sturgeon. (As a small boy in Nebraska I once saw one of those big Mississippi catfish, taken from the Missouri river. It was more than four feet long and weighed 85 pounds.)

At the mouth of the Ohio River Jolliet's men found wild geese and ducks which made no effort to fly or swim away from them, and wild turkeys which paid no attention to them. Later, when early settlers came into the Ohio Country, they easily caught wild gos-

Colonists ate few wild turkeys (left) but later breeding with domestic English cousins produced today's table bird. Its peculiar beard (detailed below) is composed of primitive, bristle-like feathers. Audubon's family group (above) is idealized as the cock often destroys eggs and poults. Habitat loss and overhunting nearly wiped out the wild turkey, but wise management brought it back.

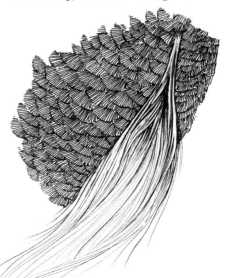

49

lings and wild turkey poults and had no trouble taming them and starting their own domesticated flocks. The Jolliet party also saw passenger pigeons and nesting trees in which most of the branches had broken under the weight of the roosting birds.

The explorers continued down the Big River until they met Indians who made it clear that they knew the white man. Then, sure the Mississippi emptied into the Gulf of Mexico, not into the Pacific, they turned back. This time they went up the Illinois River, found its valley teeming with ducks, geese, swans, parrots (Carolina parakeets), deer, wildcats, and beaver. At the headwaters they portaged back to Lake Michigan, and Jolliet headed for Quebec. In a hurry, he tried to shoot a rapid instead of portaging, his canoe was swamped and overturned, and all his records and maps were lost. Pere Marquette's records, in another canoe, were the only ones saved.

In 1680 Robert Cavelier, Sieur de la Salle, continued Jolliet's explorations, going all the way to the mouth of the Mississippi. Although Father Louis Hennepin falsely made a prior claim, La Salle's party was the first to go from the Great Lakes to the Gulf and the first to report eating bison. They found "a prodigious wild bull, lying fast in the mud of the river," and they killed and butchered it. The meat was "very relishing, full of Juice . . .

for having grazed all Summer long in those vast meadows." There also were plenty of black bears. Father Jacques Gravier, a Jesuit missionary sent to the Illinois tribe in 1688, said he saw 50 bears in a single day near the mouth of the Ohio.

La Salle makes little or no mention of passenger pigeons. Oddly, few of these early explorers did. Champlain, in 1605, wrote of an "infinite number" of pigeons he had seen along the coast of Maine, and John Josselyn reported in his *New England Rarities* (1672), "I have seen a flight of Pigeons . . . that to my thinking had neither beginning nor ending, length nor breadth, and so thick I could see no sun." Pigeons on the east coast were killed off early, but the enormous inland flocks certainly could have been seen in and over the woodlands from the Ohio River to the Gulf in the 1680s.

Indeed, this whole mid-continent area teemed with wildlife and the French laid claim to all of it. The whole Mississippi Valley, in addition to the St. Lawrence and the Great Lakes. But they still had only a few minor settlements. Quebec, founded in 1608, was in 1665 still little more than a trading post of 70 houses and 550 people. One-quarter of those were religious personnel, priests and nuns. Count Frontenac once said there were only two kinds of business in Canada, "conversion of souls and conversion of beaver."

The Spanish were busy in Florida, the Caribbean, Mexico, and the Southwest. They were reaching up the Pacific Coast with missions that actually were huge ranchos. With colonies in South America, Spain had all she could manage.

Nobody had yet seen much of the country beyond the Mississippi, the western half of today's heartland and the vast area of the Great Plains, the Rocky Mountains, the Great Basin, and the

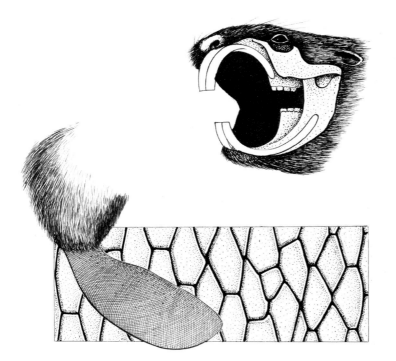

Gnaw he must, or the beaver's ever-growing teeth can grow too long and cause starvation. The tail (magnified left) serves as swimming rudder, alarm signal, and as prop for tree felling. Trapping intensified as beaver top hats became the vogue. Acknowledging its debt to American wildlife, the Hudson's Bay Company coat of arms (top) shows four beavers, a fox, and two rampant moose.

Sierra beyond. Except in the central English colonies, the fur trade dominated colonial life.

The English colonies grew swiftly, once they were past initial hardships. The woodland provided most of the materials for their livelihood and comfort—food, fuel, and shelter. Yet one of the first things the colonists did was cut down the trees. To people coming from a land where the only woodland belonged to the king and was tended and patrolled, the virgin forests were frightening. Who knew what wild animals or hostile Indians were hiding there? Even night-singing insects were alarming to European ears unaccustomed to the deafening late-summer chorus of katydids and locusts. "From the slight chirping of a few grasshoppers or crickets in England," wrote a visitor as late as 1819, "no one can have a conception of the noise of a summer night here . . . very unpleasant to (the) ears . . ." Skunks struck the newcomers as another appalling novelty. But their main motivation for the backbreaking task was to clear land for fields, for farming. So the trees were cut and the virgin forest near the settlements became the first natural resource to be systematically wiped out by the newcomers.

It was a rich land, however, and the settlers paid tribute in the names they gave it—names like Pine Springs, Elk Valley, Eagle Rock, Skunk Hollow, Hawk Mountain. However, those who described America in the seventeenth and early eighteenth centuries sometimes confused fact with hearsay. They wrote of weird monsters and fantastic landscapes.

William Bartram saw alligators in Florida swamps like Big Cypress (left) but he only imagined the "clouds of smoke issuing from his dilated nostrils" as he sketched them (far left) in 1774. A valve at the back of the throat (below) closes to keep water out when the 'gator pursues underwater prey. Similar muscles seal its ears and nostrils.

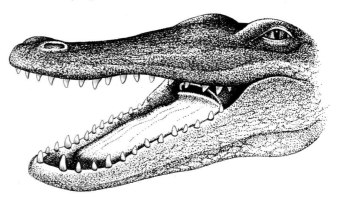

Some such fantasy is found in Josselyn's writings and even in John Lawson's 1709 *A New Voyage to Carolina.*

But by the mid-eighteenth century a new note had been sounded. Peter Kalm, Andre Michaux, Mark Catesby, and John Bartram (our first native botanist) began to write about the American wilderness, particularly in the East and South, as it really was. William Bartram, son of John and a naturalist and artist of distinction, spent four years exploring unsettled areas of the Southeast. He traveled 5,000 miles, on foot and horseback, and kept a detailed journal. Bartram's *Travels* is fascinating and full of original observation, most of it since shown to be wholly accurate. Both Bartrams were good observers and splendid reporters of what they saw.

But few of the colonists shared their keen interest in natural history at that time. As the eighteenth century passed its midpoint, the waves of political dissent became insistent and the demand for freedom from the galling restrictions of royal decrees from England overrode any other considerations. Separation from the mother country became inevitable, and war was as sure as tomorrow's sunrise.

In an oblique way, the American wilderness must be given considerable credit for the outcome of that war. The Revolution was preceded by the French and Indian War and lesser clashes between French and English interests in this country, out of which England had acquired title to Canada. But the colonists, who had been conscripted to do much of the fighting, had learned all there was to know about frontier war. Now the English were going to see what those colonists could do when they were fighting for something they wanted for themselves. They were also going to see the transformation which a century and a half of wilderness experience had wrought in their former countrymen.

The result, for these and a multitude of other reasons, was colonial victory and colonial freedom. And soon after the remarkable young colonial leaders had established the United States of America and set about the business of building an independent nation, expansion westward into the Ohio Country began.

Long before the Revolution some Americans had grown up restless, fretting under the restraints of community living. Some of these became hunters, trappers, frontiersmen—restless wanderers who had to go and see and do, some of whom later were glorified as pathfinders and guides. Daniel Boone was one of them. Boone left his native Pennsylvania, some said, as soon as he could tote a long-barreled rifle and headed for the far hills. In 1775 he led 28 axmen cutting a trail for pioneers, later known as the Wilderness Road, from Virginia through Cumberland Gap into Kentucky where he founded several settlements. Boone's Wilderness Road soon became a thoroughfare for Conestoga wagons and oxcarts rolling west. Other pioneers built flat boats and floated down the Ohio River to claim the rich farmland on the new frontier.

Before and during Boone's day the long hunters had been over the same ground. The long hunters were hunters and traders who went into the mountains of Tennessee and Kentucky, stayed at times as long as two years, and came back with packs of deerskins and furs. The records indicate that at least 80 long hunters had crossed the Alleghenies even before the Revolution.

But it still was a hunter's and trapper's paradise when the settlers began to move in, beaver and deer abounding. They were still the basic items in the young nation's fur trade. Beaver skins were used in Europe for their felting fur which was made into hats—and worn so extensively that "beaver" became common slang for hat. Deerskin breeches also had become fashionable abroad. In most of the back country here in America the settlers, too, dressed in deerskin, but used second-quality skins. A first-quality buckskin was worth a dollar, and this probably was the source of another slang expression—calling a dollar a buck.

The bald eagle represents freedom and nobility to most Americans; it lives, however, as a scavenger. The "white-headed eagle" opposite was sketched by colonial artist-naturalist Mark Catesby about 1723 in the act of stealing a mullet from an osprey. Binocular vision plus greater distance from lens to retina let the eagle scan the horizon without eye movement and plummet unerringly to its prey.

As a source of hard cash as well as meat, deer were now scarce throughout New England and some historians have compared their rapid disappearance in the southeastern states to the slaughter of the plains buffalo a century later. From 1699 to 1715 South Carolina traders alone shipped an average of 54,000 buckskins to England each year. In the peak year of 1748 they shipped 160,000 skins. Small wonder that a closed season had been established by law in all states except Georgia by 1776. Massachusetts had declared a closed season on deer as early as 1694, but it was largely ignored. Deer were a pest in the cornfield and any colonist felt he had a right to take venison to feed his family.

But there were no game laws in the Ohio Country. Settlers had to eat and they had to protect themselves. They killed turkeys and waterfowl, bears and bobcats, panthers and deer, raccoons and opossums. They weren't going to live like paupers in the wilderness. They were going to "civilize" that country. But they had first to contend with the enormous trees in the Ohio forests. Black walnut trees grew six and seven feet in diameter. Though there was little pine, there was a great deal of chestnut, and many varieties of tall, straight oak.

Sycamores were huge and the biggest of them nearly always were hollow. A big, hollow syca-

more could shelter a whole party of men—one diarist says 20 or 30 men could get into one tree. Sometimes they had first, however, to rout a family of bears. Some settlers used such sycamores as shelters for their families until they could build a log cabin. Some used them as temporary barns for their horses and cattle. Tulip poplars also grew big. Daniel Boone made a 60-foot dugout with a burden of five tons out of a single tulip poplar log.

Carving clearings out of the big woods, the settlers made room around their cabins for sun and cornfields and safety from surprise. Many of them simply girdled the trees as the Indians did and let them die. Then the sunlight could reach the ground, and they could plant corn. When he got time, the settler could cut down and burn the dead trees. Some cut the trees halfway through and waited for a good wind. The wind took down a few trees to start and they and the wind together took down the rest. It made quite a tangle, but after a while the trees were dry enough to burn where they lay.

The new growth—brush, and young trees which sprang up at the edge of the clearings—provided food for deer which were now increasing in numbers as the settlers killed off their predators, the wolves, bears, and cougars. Not so fortunate were the elk and woods bison which gathered at the salt licks and grazed in the natural meadows in the Kentucky country. The bison were darker than those of the plains and had almost no hump. They were seen in herds of more than a hundred, which to newcomers seemed remarkable, but never such herds as those common on the western plains, of hundreds of thousands. Pioneers and market hunters eliminated both the woods bison and the elk east of the Mississippi by the middle of the nineteenth century.

The early Ohio settlers were amazed at the number and size of the river fish there. The biggest were catfish weighing as much as 110 pounds. Eight-pound perch were common, and occasionally one

With claws powerful enough to rip a fallen tree for its treasure of bugs, the black bear (opposite) and the grizzly (above) were the most dangerous wildlife on the advancing frontier. Yet first Indians and then white men, ever encroaching, pushed them into remote country. Black bear still roam Appalachian ridges, but the grizzly lives only in the western mountains and Alaska.

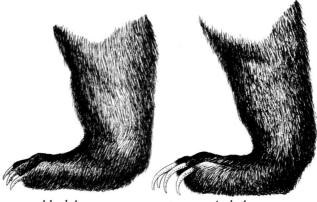

black bear   *grizzly bear*

weighing 12 pounds was caught. And for those who liked shellfish there was freshwater fare that, some said, was equal to salt-water oysters and lobster—fresh-water mussels and river crayfish which reached a length of eight inches.

Bob-white quail, then called "partridges," were netted by the hundred. Spruce grouse, stupidly tame, were common in flocks of as many as 100. When disturbed, they flew to the nearest tree or fence and let the hunter approach to within 15 or 20 paces. Those in the upper part of the tree did not fly even when birds on the lower branches were shot, thus earning the name of "fool hen."

And now, with more people moving in and settling, earlier reports of incredible flocks of passenger pigeons were verified again and again. In 1803 a pigeon roost near Marietta, Ohio, was reported to cover 1,000 acres. "The destruction of timber and brush on such large tracts of land by these small animals," one settler wrote, "is almost incredible. How many millions of them must have assembled to effect it." Repeatedly, skeptical Easterners heard how a flock of pigeons came down and ate all the mast, the beechnuts, acorns, and chestnuts on which the settlers relied as feed for their hogs. In consequence, one settler recorded succinctly, "numbers of hogs starved to death." Yet even these pigeon flocks apparently were only minor and local evidence of the really big flocks which Alexander Wilson would describe so vividly a few years later.

Back home where those settlers and their parents came from—back there in Philadelphia and then in the new capital on the Potomac where Thomas Jefferson was inaugurated in 1801—there were men in charge who knew more than a little about what was going on. George Washington had been to and beyond Pittsburgh when it still was Fort Duquesne, and almost drowned in the ice-jammed Ohio. Thomas Jefferson could tell a white oak from a red oak as far as he could see it, knew all about farming, invented a plow, and in his mind's eye kept looking beyond the Ohio Country, far across the Mississippi westward.

Men like these understood that people who were struggling through the swamps and hacking their way through the woods weren't going to be content with half a continent. Something like that must have been in the minds of those who insisted, in 1782, that the bald eagle must be our national bird. True, Ben Franklin held out for the wild turkey. But even he had to admit before he died in 1790 that this nation wasn't going to be the kind that would sit on a limb and let a hunter kill it like a "fool hen" and stew it in a pot or roast it on a spit. Nor would it run at first sight of an enemy and hide in the brush.

Meanwhile, the Mississippi River, from its source to its mouth, was being claimed and counter-claimed. The French established trading posts at New Orleans and St. Louis.

Then European wars began to shift loyalties and territories. For a time it was hard to tell who owned, or at least laid claim to, Florida, New Orleans, and the Louisiana Territory—virtually the whole of America's midlands and Gulf coast. Jefferson, by then President, knowing Napoleon probably soon would be at war with England, didn't like the prospect of English victory and English possession of Louisiana. He sent James Monroe to France to attempt to buy New Orleans and West Florida.

Jefferson shared his plans with Congress, and then told Congress he would like to send a secret expedition out west to see what was there and possibly find a trade route to what might be an important new fur area or a short route to the Pacific. Congress kept the secret and voted $2,500 to finance such a mission. Jefferson chose his personal secretary, young Meriwether Lewis, to head the expedition and sent him to Philadelphia for special training in navigation, mapmaking, and natural science. For his companion in command Lewis chose fellow Virginian and Army man William Clark, younger brother of George Rogers Clark.

Final preparations were about to begin when word came from Paris that on April 30, 1803 Napoleon had sold us the whole of the Louisiana Territory, West Florida, New Orleans and all, for $15 million. Napoleon, too, had seen that England might seize Louisiana when he went to war with her, and Napoleon chose to have the United States own it if he could at the same time disappoint and humiliate England.

Jefferson was astounded. With the stroke of a pen the territory of the United States was doubled. And now his secret mission could and would be as open as the price of fresh shad at the downtown market.

Lawson's "Beasts of Carolina" include, top to bottom, bison, rattlesnake, box turtle, rattlesnake and blacksnake, deer, bobcat, opossum, rattlesnake, gray squirrel, fish, bear, raccoon, and crab.

PAINTERS OF A
LUSH NEW LAND

*Adventurers like John Lawson sketched—and often stretched—what they saw in the
New World. Lawson knew most of the Carolina animals he drew between 1701 and
1708; yet he stunted his bison, posed snakes lashing foes with their tails, put a bobcat
on a fanciful stag, and gave his crab-catching raccoon the face of a fox.*

The manner of their fishing.

Foreground, shad, bonnet-headed shark, horseshoe crab; in the canoe, shad; background, various small fish, bonnet-headed shark, pompano, and croaker; in the sky, cormorant and possibly sea duck. Opposite: shad, female red-eyed towhee, common box turtle.

The breyling of their fish ouer t[h]e flame of fier.

WONDERS OF A RICH NEW WORLD

To John White, Roanoke colonist and later governor, the ordinary box turtle dwelt
in a dome of exquisite mosaic. In his watercolors of 1585 a cultivated grain called
maize grew ears as big as birds; a towhee took her pick of colorful kernels (odd fare
for this eater of seeds, berries, and insects). Indians, too, were part of nature's web.
As White drew shad fish "broyling," his ally Thomas Hariot noted that "These savages
preserve nothing, using everything up"—an imprudence they seemed able to afford as
they harvested teeming pompano, croakers, and horseshoe crabs.

AN EYE FOR UNIQUE FLORA AND FAUNA

From 1712 to 1726, English naturalist Mark Catesby roamed from Virginia to the Bahamas, sketching and studying wildlife, shipping specimens to sponsors in the Royal Society, and lamenting their demands for more. Back in England, he toiled another 16 years on 40 plates and text, "etching them myself" without cross-hatching, "choosing rather . . . to follow the humour of the Feathers which is more laborious." To each he added a "Description," detailing the ways of hop tree and swallowtail—and of "the charming Bedfellow," a rattlesnake, that shared his cot one night. Europe hailed his two-volume Natural History, *finally completed in 1743.*

Timber rattlesnake. Opposite: yellow tiger swallowtail and hop tree.

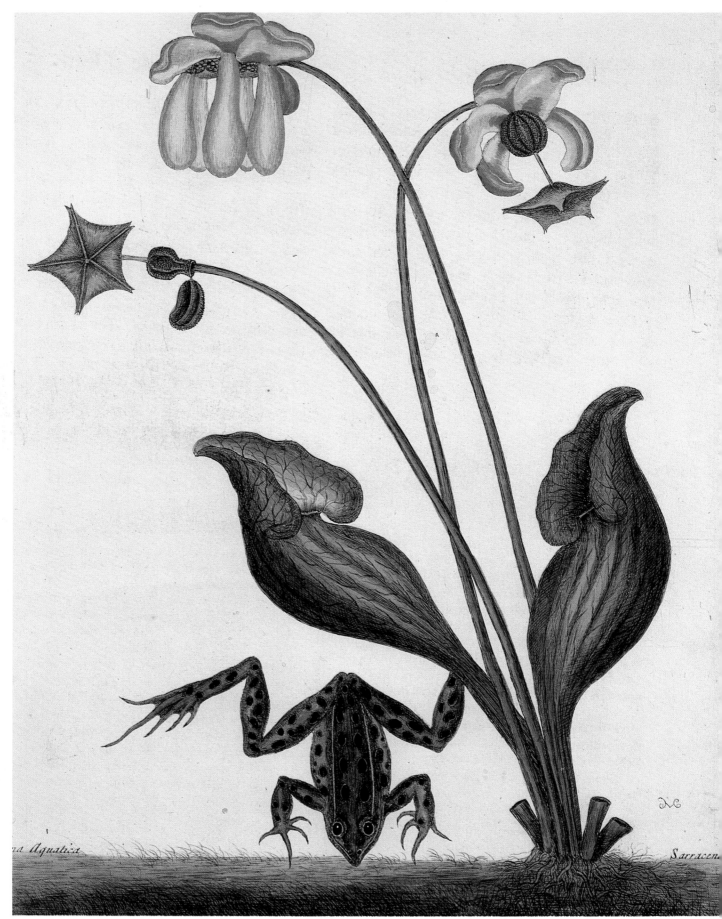

Leopard frog and pitcher plant. Opposite: eastern chipmunk with wild nutmeg, and mastic tree.

T.75.

Sciurus   Cornus

EVERYWHERE "ABOUNDING WITH . . . VARIETY"

   *It was Catesby's way to portray plants and animals in the company they keep in
nature. Opposite, a carnivorous pitcher plant shades the leaping leopard frog with whom
it shares the marshland's insects. But specimens and descriptions sent by friends still
in the colonies could wreak strange ecology. Above, a wild nutmeg from Georgia's
Gov. Oglethorpe is about to be devoured by a Virginia chipmunk 'neath a Bahamas
mastic tree. Some of Catesby's subjects mirrored cousins in the Old World, others were
to his eyes wondrously novel. Europe had lost many species when glaciers forced them
south to die out on slopes of the Alps and Pyrenees. Lacking such barriers, America
seemed to Europeans an endless Eden.*

"I HAVE SERIOUSLY BEGUN . . ."

Alexander Wilson would not live to see its end, but in 1806 he launched a monumental project: He would record, in words and colored plates, every bird found in America. "I have resigned every other amusement, except reading and fiddling," the young Scottish teacher wrote to his friend, American artist-naturalist William Bartram. To shave costs, Wilson, like Catesby, learned to make his own engravings, and grouped as many as six birds on a plate. Thus, in his 1808-14, nine-volume American Ornithology, *hummingbirds and a towhee listen to the mockingbird while warblers eye a Carolina parakeet—probably Wilson's pet, "Poll."*

Top to bottom, mockingbird, ruby-throated hummingbirds, towhee and egg; above, portrait of Wilson by R. Peale. Opposite: top to bottom, Carolina parakeet and hooded, Canada, and Wilson's warblers.

Left to right, Louisiana heron, American oyster-catcher, whooping crane, and long-billed curlew. Opposite: clockwise, blue mountain and hemlock warblers (hypothetical species seen only by Wilson), and passenger pigeon; ivory-billed and pileated woodpeckers.

EARLY WARNINGS OF COMING DISASTER

For seven years Wilson labored on a task that must have seemed endless. He collected specimens on spare time trips to Maine, New Orleans, Ohio; his friend Meriwether Lewis brought him more from the Far West. Amid such abundance, who could foretell extinction? But as he studied the ivory-billed woodpecker, Wilson realized that its niche in deep forests along fertile river bottoms, where great dead trees harbored the beetle larvae it fed upon, would surely fall to ax and plow. He watched passenger pigeons stream overhead, estimating one flock at some two billion birds, yet saw the flocks already beginning to shrink. His stately whooping crane's numbers later plunged to 14, and have risen only to 81 today. Wilson erred when he forecast the pileated woodpecker's demise, but with pigeon—and probably ivory-bill—he painted what we will never see.

A WILDLIFE MASTER, IN FIELD OR STUDIO

When John James Audubon began his great works depicting the continent's birds and mammals (1827-1845), the East was already losing much wildlife. Gray squirrels could still be observed from his window, but other animals were shot in the field and brought back to the studio—which may account for the contorted posture of his fox. Still other species (above) were spied at home.

Eastern gray squirrel; above, house mouse. Opposite: gray fox.

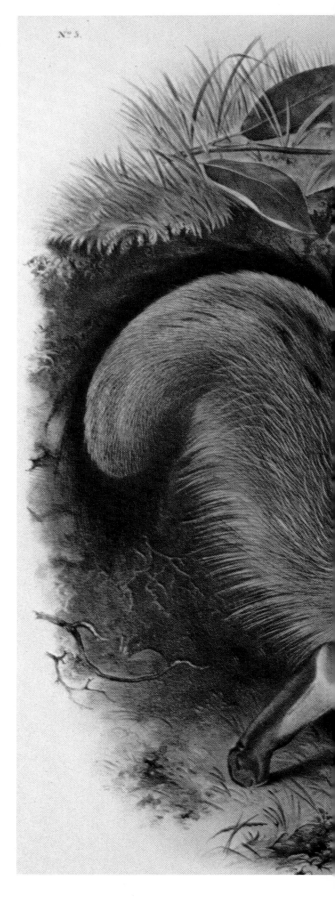

PLATE XXI.

Wagon Wheels
Follow
Buffalo Trails

The Lewis and Clark expedition, 35 soldiers and nine civilians organized in military fashion, left St. Louis May 14, 1804. They started up the Missouri River in a 55-foot keelboat which could be propelled by sail, oars, or tow rope, and two smaller "perioques", heading for North Dakota, where they would spend the first winter.

Explorers, traders, and trappers had been up the Missouri at least as far as the Dakotas, but few of them had brought back much information about the land or its wildlife. Vagrants, fugitives, squaw-men, and various anonymous wanderers had also gone up the river and even out onto the plains to live among the Indians, but naturally they had made no reports. One exception was Pierre Antoine Tabeau whom Lewis and Clark would meet near the Arikara villages in the Dakotas, but his journal was a minor record.

The expedition found some kinds of game had already been killed off or had left the lower valley in Missouri and Nebraska. They saw no buffalo there, the big herds having migrated to their summer range in the short-grass country of the northern Great Plains. There were no grizzly bears. Grizzlies had been fairly common on the prairies only a few years earlier but as hunting and settlement increased, the big "white bears" had retreated upriver. Yet birds were everywhere. They saw few sandhill cranes but there were many pelicans on the islands in the Missouri, and flocks of Carolina parakeets, bright green with red or yellow or orange markings on their heads. The parakeets were not good eating, so they survived until the middle of the century when the settlers killed them off to protect their orchards. Lewis and Clark saw numerous flocks of sage grouse, quail, wild turkeys, and prairie chickens along the lower part of the river. And they saw thousands of wild geese and ducks.

Deer were common except on the Nebraska plains. Up the river from there the Lewis and Clark party had all the venison and beaver tails they wanted. Lewis especially liked the taste of beaver tail which was regarded as a delicacy by some trappers and frontiersmen.

The Lewis and Clark party required "4 deer, an Elk and a deer, or one buffaloe" every day, and they experienced no shortage of meat until they began to cross the Rockies the next spring. They killed

Flushed from cover like the mule deer above, prairie wildlife fascinated explorers and frontier artists. Titian Peale portrayed the black-tailed deer opposite and the male prairie chicken (right) in 1819 and 1820. Spring is the time to see the prairie chicken's courting antics— such as the strutting cock opposite, ready to fight for hens' favors.

The pronghorn's speed amazed Lewis and Clark; it can better a mile a minute. Vast herds then roamed the prairies (bottom), their fawns seeking sage brush cover from eagle and coyote (right). A danger signal is given by a male sentry (below), his eyesight as good as a man's with binoculars. His white rump hair seems luminous when it rises to flash the message: Flee!

their first buffalo in what now is the southeast corner of South Dakota. From there on, the expedition saw more and more of them. Having no idea of how many there might be in a "gangue," as they called a herd, they were at first surprised to see 500 in one such massive gathering.

Near Great Falls in Montana, Lewis wrote later in his journal:

"... it is now the season at which the buffaloe begin to coppelate and the bulls keep a tremendous roaring we could hear them for many miles and there are such numbers of them that there is one continual roar ... when I arrived in sight of the white-bear Islands the missouri bottoms on both sides of the river were crouded with buffaloe I sincerely beleif that there were not less than 10 thousand buffaloe within a circle of 2 miles arround that place."

Lewis was not exaggerating. Reliable estimates of the total number of buffalo on the Great Plains when the white men first saw them set the figure at between 50,000,000 and 60,000,000.

With such enormous herds, both whites and Indians wasted much of the meat. The "fleeces," the fat, tender meat on each side of the spine, were the choice parts. This included the hump, regarded as the best meat of all. Often only the fleeces were taken, and the tongue, which was a special delicacy. The rest of the carcass was left for the bears or the wolves.

Scientifically, of course, the animal called "buffalo" in America is a bison. True buffalo are large, straight-backed animals native to Africa and Asia.

The expedition also had its first sight of pronghorn antelopes, which they called goats. The pronghorn actually is distantly related to the goat and definitely is not an antelope. It is estimated that once there were as many as 40,000,000 pronghorns in America, most of them roaming the plains country with the vast herds of buffalo. They, too, migrated with the seasons, for though they could withstand extremes of heat and cold—a temperature range of close to 145 degrees—snow was a deadly enemy. It hampered the pronghorn's fleetness in flight, its chief protection from predators. The pronghorn's one weakness is curiosity. A hunter lying on the ground with his hat on the end of his upright gun barrel will lure a pronghorn within

rifle range. A red bandanna tied to a stick will do the same thing.

Yet pronghorns have a highly effective alarm system. As the herd grazes, several sentries remain on the alert. If a potential enemy approaches—and pronghorns have phenomenally good eyesight—a sentinel snorts and flashes the alarm, literally flashes it. The animal has a large rump patch of white hair that can be erected at will; when erected the alarm is flashed, and every pronghorn in sight takes off, so fast that they seem to fly.

Their natural predators, chiefly wolves and coyotes, cannot catch pronghorns except when they are very young or very old or injured. It was man, both Indian and white, who was responsible for the losses of the great pronghorn flocks in the nineteenth century. Fencing, competition with domestic animals, and overhunting reduced the herds to a small fraction of their original size.

In South Dakota the expedition also saw prairie dogs for the first time. Prairie dogs are not dogs at all, but rodents, cousins of the squirrels. Their underground communities are sometimes incredibly widespread. The biggest prairie dog town I ever heard of was reported on the high plains of Texas by Vernon Bailey who was with the U.S. Biological Survey from 1887 to 1933 and became its chief field naturalist. That town extended 250 miles in length, 100 miles in breadth, and was estimated to have 400,000,000 prairie dogs in it. The prairie dog towns which Lewis and Clark saw probably covered at most a square mile each. In such a town the animals dig straight down three feet or more to an elaborate network of underground runways. The entrance holes, spaced ten feet or so apart, are mounded with a raised, doughnut-like lip that keeps rainwater from flooding the burrows. Unfortunately for the prairie dogs, their fortress towns cannot keep out their mortal enemies, the rattlesnake, bullsnake, badger, black-footed ferret, and the burrowing owl.

During the summer the Lewis and Clark expedition had its problems with insects, as all travelers did on the inland rivers and lakes. Horseflies, the big green-headed gadflies, tortured both men and animals. So did the big river-bottom mosquitoes. Gen. Hiram Chittenden, an army civil engineer writing later of his frontier experiences, declared:

"[*The mosquito*] *abounded everywhere except upon the naked prairie, and was particularly numerous in those places which were most frequented by man, the river valleys and the forests which lined the streams . . . Strange as it may seem, their strength and voracity increase . . . the farther north they are met . . . it destroys the aim of the rifle, interferes with the explorer when making important observations, causes the pilot to let slip his wheel in dangerous places, to say nothing of destroying sleep and so inflaming the skin as to unfit one for work. Of all the pests of the prairies the mosquito was incomparably the worst.*"

The expedition had no trouble with bees. Honeybees were just beginning to move up the Missouri. They were not native but had been brought from Europe by early settlers. There were none west of the Mississippi until 1797, but they moved westward about ten miles a year. By 1809 "bee trees" with good stores of honey were found 600 miles up the Missouri from St. Louis.

The exploring party also saw the long-tailed black-and-white magpies, unknown in the East. Magpies are beautiful birds with raucous voices. The men captured four of them, kept them in cages all winter, and sent them back east to President Jefferson. Jefferson was fond of birds and kept a tame mockingbird in the White House.

The expedition went into winter quarters near the mouth of the Knife River in North Dakota. They built a structure of cottonwood logs and named it Fort Mandan for the Indian tribe in that area. After an untroubled winter the expedition struck out into virtually unexplored territory, leaving Fort Mandan on April 7.

They now were in grizzly bear country. Although the men had fired at one in October, they still knew little about grizzlies. Trappers for the Hudson's Bay

"Petits chiens," French explorers called them, but prairie dogs are really rodents whose labyrinthine tunnels aerate and improve the soil. Sod house settlers deplored their deep holes as hazards to livestock, but children—this book's author Hal Borland among them— spent hours watching them pop in and out, bark their danger signals, and settle their spats in 30 seconds.

In a land of few trees, birds also live on or in the ground. The native burrowing owl (left), claims squatter's rights to an abandoned prairie dog tunnel.

Company had told of hair-raising encounters with "a Bear wch is Bigger than any white Bear and is Neither White nor Black But silver hair'd like our English Rabbit." Alexander Mackenzie, the Scottish-born Canadian explorer and fur trader, had said the Indians showed "great apprehension of this kind of bear, which is called the grisly bear." Although Lewis and Clark, too, had been hearing Indian accounts of grizzlies, the explorers were skeptical. Then, not far up the river from winter quarters, they found the biggest bear tracks they had ever seen, footprints 11 inches long and seven and a half inches broad. Lewis wrote in his journal that these bears must be "extreemly wary and shy" and the whole expedition was "anxious to meet with some of these bears."

On April 29, 1805 Lewis and one companion, on shore alone, ran into two grizzlies. Overconfident, both men fired at once. Luckily, only one of the wounded bears attacked. The other fled. The two men ran for their lives, trying to get powder and ball into their muzzle-loading rifles. Finally they reloaded and killed the bear and found it was only a half-grown male. A few days later they saw a fully-grown grizzly out on a sandbar where everyone could shoot at it. It took ten bullets to knock it down and kill it. Then Lewis admitted that grizzlies were, as he put it, "hard to die." The muzzle-loaders of the early nineteenth century lacked the velocity, the shocking-power, of modern weapons. Even a shot to the heart did not immediately kill a grizzly, and the brain was protected by flesh and a thick frontal bone. Only twice did the expedition kill a grizzly bear with one shot.

As the expedition fought the river "uphill" across Montana and into the Rockies, they were amazed to see "a large herd of the Bighorned anamals", Rocky Mountain bighorn sheep. The sheep leaped and ran along sheer cliffs where it appeared nothing could find a foothold. But they kept to the heights and the party's meat-hunters shot very few of them. Later travelers shot a great many.

By then they were in the heart of some of the best beaver country in North America, which soon would be worked over by the mountain men. Clark, looking into the side streams as they advanced, reported that beaver dams succeeded each other at short distances as far as the eye could see.

They reached the headwaters of the Missouri between present-day Bozeman and Butte barely in time to switch to pack horses for the difficult crossing of the Continental Divide before winter could hem them in. On the last lap of the trip down the Pacific slope, at times the party was reduced to a diet of horse meat, coyote meat, and crows. At one point they tried the Nez Perce diet of roots and dried salmon which made everyone in the expedition sick.

They built Fort Clatsop near present-day Astoria, Oregon, and settled in for the winter. The next

The report of official explorers Lewis and Clark confirmed the wisdom of Jefferson's Louisiana Purchase. They found a land rich in wildlife, including such unknown species as the "cock of the plains," the sage grouse sketched in Clark's elk-bound field book below. The first published account of the 1804-1806 expedition shows "Captain Clark and his men shooting Bears" (opposite below). The grizzly, more accurately portrayed by Leigh in 1912 (opposite above), dines on grubs, grasses, berries, small mammals, and fish when not contending with men.

spring they returned much the way they had come, arriving in St. Louis September 23, 1806 with the first reports ever made of that far western country.

Of particular interest was Lewis' list of the animals they had seen and identified from the Rocky Mountains to the Pacific Ocean:

"... the native wild animals, consisting of the Brown white or grizly bear, (which I beleive to be the same family with a mearly accedental difference in point of colour) the black bear, the common red deer, the black tailed fallow deer, the Mule deer, Elk, the large brown wolf, the small woolf of the plains, the large wolf of the plains, the tiger cat, the common red fox, black fox or fisher, silver fox, large red fox of the plains, small fox of the plains or kit fox, Antelope, sheep, beaver, common otter, sea Otter, mink, spuck, seal, raccoon, large grey squirrel, small brown squirrel, small grey squirrel, ground squirrel, sewelel, Braro, rat, mouse, mole, Panther, hare, rabbit, and polecat or skunk."

But of all the wildlife they discovered and described, only two birds now bear their names: Clark's nutcracker and Lewis' woodpecker.

Next came the colorful era of the mountain men, trappers and traders who followed Lewis and Clark's route into the northern Rockies to explore and exploit that rich fur country from 1806 to 1840. Until that time the organized fur trade of the continent had been dominated by the Hudson's Bay Company which had been founded in 1670; its first major rival, the Northwest Company which was organized in 1787; and by their leading rival in the States, the American Fur Company founded by John Jacob Astor in 1808. Astor's firm brought great tonnages of beaver, mink, marten, fisher, otter, weasel, muskrat, and wolf pelts out of the forests of the Great Lakes region and the

Up the Missouri and into the high country went the trappers of the 1820s seeking valuable pelts. These mountain men developed a distinctive look and style, captured in the watercolor opposite by Danish artist Olaf Seltzer. Indians carried buffalo hides to forts for trade as depicted by Seltzer's friend Charles Russell in his watercolor "The Robe Traders" (upper right).

The thick undercoat of the beaver (lower photo) made it a prime target for trappers, but muskrat (upper photo) and other fur-bearing mammals were taken as well.

Mississippi Valley. Astor's Pacific Fur Company succeeded in beating the Canadians to the rich China trade by establishing a trading post at the mouth of the Columbia River in 1811, only to lose it to the British in 1814. Nevertheless when he switched from the declining fur business to real estate in 1834, Astor had created the first U.S. business monopoly and had directed the biggest commercial enterprise in the United States up to that time.

One of the first mountain men to get into the lucrative fur business was Manuel Lisa, a Spaniard born in New Orleans. Lisa went up the Missouri in 1807 and built a trading post at the mouth of the Bighorn in Montana. From then until 1820 he was up and down the Missouri River every year and the Missouri Fur Company which he headed had a steady business on the upper river. Lisa and other early mountain men were preceded in the Rockies only by an official army exploration led by Col. Zebulon Pike through Colorado and New Mexico in 1806. In 1819 the Army sent Maj. Stephen Long to explore the area between the Missouri River and the Rockies.

The War of 1812 interrupted western exploration for a time, but by 1822 William H. Ashley, lieutenant governor of Missouri, and Andrew Henry had organized the Rocky Mountain Fur Company and enlisted one of history's most remarkable bands of young frontiersmen. In the group were Jedediah Smith, Dave Jackson, Will Sublette and his brother Milton, Mike Fink, Hugh Glass, Jim Bridger, Tom Fitzpatrick, and Jim Beckwourth. Andrew Henry led them up the river first in 1822 and lost a keelboat with a cargo worth $10,000. Then in 1823 Ashley had serious trouble with the Indians, but established a post at the mouth of the Yellowstone on the North Dakota-Montana border. In 1824 they had good fortune at last. The business, primarily trade in beaver skins, became so profitable that Ashley sold his share and retired in 1826, a rich man. In 1831 Missouri sent him to Congress where he was a forceful advocate of western development.

At first trappers had to take their peltry all the way from the mountains to St. Louis by packhorse and riverboat. Then in 1825 Ashley proposed a summer "rendezvous" on the Green River in southwest Wyoming, a rude trade fair to which he brought from St. Louis beads, bright-colored cloth, and trinkets as well as trapping gear, sugar, tobacco, and liquor. The rendezvous became a movable annual event lasting two or three weeks, a glorified country fair with trimmings. It was legitimate trade plus drunken revels and brawls. Hundreds of Indians came, as well as white trappers. At the end of the first rendezvous, the traders loaded 8,829 pounds of beaver skins worth $50,000 on their pack horses and went back to St. Louis. A few years later when they found they could take wagons over South Pass in west central Wyoming, they doubled the number of beaver skins they bought. They also, unknowingly, opened the way that became the Oregon Trail.

The beaver trade continued until the market fell sharply in the late 1830s, when English hatters found high silk hats were easier to make than hats of beaver felt. Silk hats were soon fashionable, beavers were "out," and the cry, "Hell's full of high silk hats!" went up from the far mountains. The fur companies turned their attention to buffalo. The beaver streams were almost trapped out anyway, and there was a growing demand for buffalo skins for robes and overcoats. In 1840 the successor to the Rocky Mountain Fur Company shipped 67,000 buffalo skins down the Missouri.

When the beaver trade was still flourishing, however, the mountain men made a valuable contribution to the nation's growth by exploring much of the still unknown West. John Colter, who had gone west with Lewis and Clark and stayed to trap and explore, became the first white man to see the hot springs and other wonders along the Yellowstone.

Jedediah Smith crossed the Sierra in winter, the first white man ever to do that, and explored the Pacific coast almost to the mouth of the Columbia. Jim Bridger discovered Great Salt Lake. Kit Carson was all over the mountains, and served as guide to John C. Fremont, the self-styled "Pathfinder," leading him safely over the trails the Indians and the trappers had used for years.

Also struggling through rugged mountain passes after a long trek across arid plains came the Mormons under Brigham Young, finally pushing their cartloads of gear down into the valley of the Great Salt Lake in 1847. There they plowed and planted and grew crops which were all but destroyed by a scourge of long-horned grasshoppers, commonly called Mormon crickets today. At the crucial moment in 1848, a flight of sea gulls arrived, presumably from Great Salt Lake, ate the insects, and saved the crops. Today a beautiful sea gull monument stands near the Mormon Tabernacle in Salt Lake City, commemorating the providential event.

Along with these early trailblazers came more sophisticated wilderness travelers—artists, writers, and scientists eager to study and record the life of the fabulous West. Back in 1819 the Long expedition had been accompanied by the artist Titian Peale and the naturalist Thomas Say. Peale brought back two grizzly cubs for the Philadelphia Zoo, and Say, a

European scientists and artists also followed Lewis and Clark onto the prairies. One was the German Prince Maximilian, an amateur naturalist who brought along a young Swiss artist Karl Bodmer. It was probably in North Dakota in 1834 that Bodmer painted the Hidatsa dancer opposite. The dancer's pointed feathers and taut stature mirror the attitude of the sage grouse below. The male grouse takes this pose when courting, its feet stamping out a double-step and its driving wings beating out the characteristic drumming sound.

zoologist and entomologist, brought back detailed information about western American insects. In 1832 George Catlin had left Philadelphia to paint Indians and did a prodigious job: 470 of his full-length portraits and some 700 sketches survive. And by 1835 Washington Irving had written *A Tour of the Prairies*, a rather superficial book on his brief trip to the plains country. In 1836 with Pierre Irving he wrote *Astoria* based on papers and reports furnished by John Jacob Astor, and in 1837, he published *The Adventures of Captain Bonneville*.

In 1846 Francis Parkman the historian made a trip west and wrote *The Oregon Trail*, still a classic. Parkman had the foresight to say that the vast herds of buffalo were doomed and that loss of the buffalo would threaten the existence of the Plains Indians.

The West and its wildlife had caught the public fancy, and works such as these were beginning to shape American life and thought. The young nation's image of itself was further expanded and buoyed in 1848 when we fought and won the Mexican War. With the acquisition of California and other western lands the United States was at last a coast-to-coast nation.

An earlier wilderness observer was Alexander Wilson, a Scottish-born Philadelphian who had conceived the idea of writing and illustrating a book about America's birds and set out in 1806 to sketch them in the wild. Wilson's work ran to nine volumes and was so thorough that in the next 100 years only 23 indigenous land birds were added to his list for eastern United States north of Florida.

In 1810 Wilson saw a flock of passenger pigeons in Kentucky flying overhead "at a height beyond gunshot ... from right to left far as the eye could reach" for five hours. He estimated the total number of pigeons in that flight to be 2,230,272,000, and he cal-

Passenger pigeon numbers astounded early naturalists like Audubon, who caught their graceful beauty (above) in his 1830 Birds of America. *Pigeons were slaughtered for sport, for sale as meat, and to protect cleared fields as in the Iowa farm scene at right. Land clearing eventually destroyed hardwood forests—especially beech trees—which the birds needed for food and cover. Malnutrition and resultant diseases helped finish them off.*

A reminder of this bird we will never see is its close relative, the mourning dove (opposite above).

culated that if each consumed half a pint of mast a day "the whole quantity at this rate would equal 17,424,000 bushels per day!"

Wilson's description of the great flocks of passenger pigeons is a classic:

"The most remarkable characteristic of these birds is their associating together, both in their migrations and also during the period of incubation, in such prodigious numbers as almost to surpass belief . . . These migrations appear to be undertaken rather in quest of food, than merely to avoid the cold of the climate, since we find them lingering in the northern regions around Hudson's Bay so late as December . . . I have witnessed these migrations in the Genessee country—often in Pennsylvania, and also in various parts of Virginia, with amazement; but all that I had then seen of them were mere straggling parties, when compared with the congregated millions which I have since beheld in our western forests, in the states of Ohio, Kentucky, and the Indiana territory. These fertile and extensive regions abound with the nutritious beech nut, which constitute the chief food of the Wild Pigeon . . . It sometimes happens that having consumed the whole produce of the beech trees in an extensive district, they discover another at the distance perhaps of sixty or eighty miles, to which they regularly repair every morning and return as regularly . . . in the evening, to their . . . roosting place . . . The ground is covered to the depth of several inches with their dung; all the tender grass and underwood destroyed; the surface strewed with large limbs of trees broken down by the weight of the birds . . . and the trees themselves, for thousands of acres, killed as completely as if girdled with an axe."

The total number of pigeons in America could only be guessed, but it certainly was well into the billions, probably the largest number of birds of one species ever known in one country or even on one continent. They were shot, netted, clubbed, killed in every way possible, and they were sent to city markets by the barrel and by the railroad carload. In the market they sold for as little as 12¢ a dozen. As demand for them waned, they were fed to the hogs which had been deprived of the mast consumed by the birds.

John James Audubon traveled extensively up and down the Mississippi, Ohio, and Missouri Rivers between 1810 and 1826, gaining knowledge and experience he would need for his books. After observing one pigeon slaughter, he said, "Persons unacquainted with these birds might naturally conclude that such havock would soon put an end to the species. But I have satisfied myself, by long observation, that nothing but the gradual diminution of our forests can accomplish this decrease."

Mr. Audubon's remark was prophetic. He died in 1851, and only about 25 years later the last big pigeon nesting, estimated at around 136,000,000 birds, occurred in central Michigan. While market hunters from all over the country devastated that enormous gathering, it was the steady clear-cutting of the hardwood forests which had concentrated flocks into pitifully small remnants of their habitat. Oddly enough, the Chicago Fire of 1871 indirectly speeded their demise when the forests of the Lake States were turned into lumber to rebuild the city. Malnutrition and disease thinned the few remaining flocks. A few pigeons were kept in captivity, but they failed to reproduce.

Despised by ranchers, the wolf and coyote fared badly as land was settled. The timber wolf (below), maligned in folklore and art, is in fact a valuable predator. At right these social animals pause from hunting for a romp on a snow-covered lake. The coyote has resisted human encroachment better, and its range continues to increase, chiefly because it also eats rodents, insects, and plant fruits. The coyotes opposite tug at the carcass of another prairie mammal that leapt successfully across wave after wave of American pioneers—the jackrabbit.

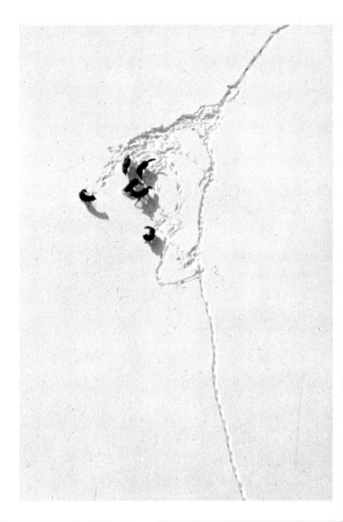

Public uneasiness over the wholesale slaughter of birds was expressed in various ways for more than 50 years before the last wild pigeon died in the Cincinnati Zoo in 1914. The first law against spring shooting of wood ducks, black ducks, woodcocks, and snipe was passed in Rhode Island as early as 1846. Eight years before that New York had outlawed the use of "batteries," multiple guns, on boats in hunting waterfowl. Both laws were subsequently repealed, but public debate over how to deal with surplus and scarcity of wildlife had begun.

In 1836 Ralph Waldo Emerson helped lay a foundation for that debate by publishing his first important essay, entitled *Nature*. It advanced the philosophy of conservation long before the word was coined. Emerson was a friend of Henry David Thoreau, who at the time was living in the little house he had built on Emerson's property near Walden Pond and was keeping the journal from which he later wrote *Walden*.

With both naturalists and men of letters articulating their concerns, small groups of conservationists grew more vociferous. One by one, state legislatures met their demands for protection for one or more species of wildlife. Between 1851 and 1864 eleven states passed laws against killing nongame birds. Even in the West, shrinking herds of big game caused closed-season laws to be enacted for the first time. In 1852 California established its first closed season to protect pronghorns and elk. In 1861 Nevada legislated a closed season on mountain sheep and mountain goats. In 1864 Idaho passed a closed-season law protecting buffalo, deer, elk, pronghorns, bighorn sheep, and mountain goats from February to July.

But there still were no closed seasons on the Great Plains. The tide of immigrants to the Oregon Country encountered tremendous herds of buffalo and to a large extent lived on their meat. They broke up some of the vast herds with often needless killing, angering the once-friendly Indians and unwittingly fulfilling Francis Parkman's prophecy.

As the Plains Indians became more and more hostile toward the whites who were also taking their land, Parkman's appraisal of the almost symbiotic relationship between Indian and buffalo became basic to unofficial government policy. It seldom was stated so bluntly, but it boiled down to a belief that one way to bring the hostile Indians to terms was by killing off the buffalo. This couldn't be done overnight, but events elsewhere would soon add momentum to the tragic drama.

The Mexican War had transferred title to California to the United States, but the leisurely rancho life persisted. *Vaqueros* still lassoed grizzlies for sport and sometimes captured grizzlies and brought them down from the mountains for bloody arena combats with longhorn steers. Only a few settlers

from the East had moved in when Jim Marshall, deepening the tailrace for a sawmill water wheel near Sutter's Fort, found nuggets of gold. That was in January, 1848. By early 1849 the rush was on.

Gold-seekers came from the Midwest by wagon and on horseback. From the East some took ship to Panama, went afoot across the isthmus, and found passage on up the coast. Others sailed around Cape Horn. They went any way they could to get to California and pick up those nuggets. Those who crossed the plains on the California Trail saw countless herds of buffalo, were halted by them, were awed by them, were angered by them. They saw the Indians who, becoming more resentful, raided the forty-niners' wagons, stole their oxen and mules and horses.

But there was no stopping the westward wave.

Another ten years and another gold discovery, this one in the mountains of Colorado, set off a second tide of adventurers across the plains. Once more the vast herds of buffalo interfered with travel and the swift-riding Indians raided, killed, and looted. White leaders met with various tribal chieftains, parleyed, tried to work out peaceful solutions. The land was to be the Indians' forever, "as long as the grass grew and the rivers ran," with only this road and that trail open to the White Father's children so they could safely go from the East to the West. Promises had been made, and treaties signed, but whites broke them.

Did not the grass still grow? Did not the rivers still run? Indian resentment boiled over, blood flowed. Though they didn't know what it meant, the Indians also resented the presence of survey parties that laid out the route of what was to become the first transcontinental railroad. Actual completion would be delayed until 1869, after the Civil War, but the railroad, the covered wagons which came before and after it, and the telegraph poles already marching across the nation, together set in motion irreversible changes for every living thing in that vast western province.

The buffalo as a free-roaming animal would be the first to go. The grizzlies that had followed the buffalo herds north and south with the seasons had already taken to the mountains to live on deer, elk, and lesser game. Wolves and coyotes remained with the buffalo, living on the young, the sick, and the very old. Some would turn to the herds of cattle and sheep that would soon graze the old buffalo ranges, but most of the coyotes and many of the wolves would eventually resort to rabbits and other small game.

Jackrabbits, however, would not easily be displaced. Both the white-tailed ones and the black-tailed ones which actually are hares travel at high speeds, progressing by tremendous leaps despite their weight of seven to ten pounds. Twenty-foot leaps are not unusual. Every few leaps the jackrabbit springs as much as six feet above the ground and looks around to see where the pursuer is.

While the plow and the crops which grow behind it could increase the rabbits' numbers, future farmers and gardeners would bring death by poisoning to untold millions of prairie dogs. The age-old balance between prairie dogs and their enemies would be almost completely wrecked. Many of those snakes, badgers, black-footed ferrets, and kit foxes would find other prey, some of it domestic. The rest would die and be no more.

The birds of the high plains would know little change until the settlers moved in. Then cultivated fields would replace the natural food and cover which had for so long made this a paradise for the prairie chicken, the sharp-tailed grouse, and the sage hen. The buffalo bird would gradually become known as the cowbird. Then as now, it laid its eggs in other birds' nests, but for a while longer it would live on and with the buffalo, eating the insects stirred from the grass by the wandering herds. The western meadowlark would sing its age-old songs while nighthawks seined the sky at dusk, and courted with that amazing display of roaring dives and swift climbs on scimitar wings.

That tremendous inland province, the short-grass plains that reach from the Gulf shore of Texas well into Canada, had been largely explored by 1860 and was ready for final conquest and settlement, first by the ranchmen, then by the homesteaders. But before that could happen there was a war to be fought, a brutal, bloody Civil War. The years 1861 to 1865 were war years for the people, but years of respite for the deer, the buffalo, and the pronghorn. For them and for many others, destiny was only marking time.

"Bulls" by T. R. Peale, 1820.

LORD
OF THE PLAINS

*Once he was lord of the grass, nodding serenely as he cropped the sprawling plains.
Early artists drew the animal poorly, as did Titian Peale in this first known
portrait of bison on the Great Plains. Perhaps the great beast seemed a
creature of the imagination, head too huge and hindquarters too puny for an animal
that weighed a ton and ran at 30 miles an hour. Today only thousands survive—
and the thundering millions of yesteryear seem indeed imaginary.*

PEACE AMID PLENTY, WAR IN ITS SEASON

Cool water sluices down dry throats in great gurgling draughts. It soothes pest-ridden hides and bids the buzzing flies begone. At river's edge it greens the succulent grass that tempts the grazers' idle nibble. The bison are at peace with themselves, with the distant elk in artist Karl Bodmer's 1833 idyll, and—so far—with the men who have named this the Missouri River and made it theirs in the Louisiana Purchase. The East's small herds have vanished, a few of their trails from meadow to meadow surviving as wagon roads that will one day know the automobile. No horns but their own yet shatter the bison's calm as bulls duel for dominance in the late-summer rut. With a charge that can splinter a two-by-twelve, a bull wins the right to mate, siring by strength a vigorous progeny.

"Herds of Bison and Elk on the Upper Missouri" by Karl Bodmer, 1833. Opposite: "Rutting Season" by Philip Russell Goodwin, 1901.

NATURE TRIMS AN
ANCIENT BALANCE

Heat and drought turn the prairie grass brown, tinder-dry. Then a growling cloud s
a spark of lightning and rolls it down the wind—which fans it to a holocaust at aweso
speed. Now the ground thunders as pronghorns, coyotes, bison in tens of thousands

"Herd of Buffalo Fleeing from Prairie Fire" by Meyer Strauss, 1888. Courtesy Amon Carter Museum, Fort Worth, Texas.

race with death, old fears forgotten as prey and predator flee side by side. Some survive, perhaps by swimming a river the flames cannot jump. Slowly the blackened wastes grow green again—and again turn black with bison.

95

FULL OF YEARS, A MONARCH FALLS

When he was five he challenged other bulls for a mate, and won. When he was 12 other bulls challenged him, bluffing with threat postures, ramming head-to-head, bellowing, stomping, raking with sturdy horns—then turning broadside to walk away in defeat from a magnificent bull in his prime. But now his 30 years cloud his eyes, corrode his joints, sap his stamina. And now the prairie wolves single him out, surround him as he lags behind the herd, befuddle him with their milling and circling and stalling as the herd grazes off. Suddenly a wolf lunges at his ear. A second snaps at his snout, a third his foreleg. His horn skewers one, his hoof cripples another—but his hind legs feel the stab of the predators' teeth tearing the tendons, laming him for the kill. About 1829 Peter Rindisbacher, young artist of the northern plains, sketched the fury of the opening attack (opposite). Around 1832 George Catlin froze another fallen monarch's final respite (below) as the wolves lick their wounds and ready for the end.

"White Wolves Attacking a Buffalo Bull" by George Catlin, c. 1832. Opposite: "Buffalo and Prairie Wolves' by Peter Rindisbacher, c. 1829.

P. Rindisbacher. Pinx.ᵗ   Lith. of Endicott & Swett.

THE INDIAN, A HUMAN PREDATOR

Two thousand centuries before man discovered America, bison roamed the continent—massive beasts then, with horns spanning seven feet. Ancient Indians hunted a smaller species by learning to stampede herds over a cliff. In its place the modern bison—smaller still—multiplied to perhaps 60,000,000 and gave the Indian meat, hides for warmth and shelter, horns for tools and talismans. Astride the white man's horse, the Indian could surround whole herds, as shown in Catlin's painting. Such a hunt in autumn should yield meat for the winter, but if supplies ran low, hungry hunters donned snowshoes and herded the animals into drifts. Catlin caught the action, and Frederic Remington the tedious aftermath as women butcher by moonlight—under the "Hungry Moon" that bade a village hunt or starve.

"Hungry Moon" by Frederic Remington, 1900. Opposite: top to bottom, "Buffalo Hunt, Surround" and "Dying Buffalo Bull, in a Snow Drift" by George Catlin, c. 1832.

ENDLESS HERDS WHOSE END WAS NEAR

They could hold up the white man's iron horse all day as they crossed its rails in plodding thousands. They had earned the right; railroads were often built along buffalo trails, since the heavy animals always sought routes with the easiest gradients. But placid herds like the one in N. H. Trotter's canvas could not hold up the white man's westering waves, nor stay the thirst for gain that lured him on. The next train's windows might bristle with rifle muzzles as some men killed for fun or trainmen for food. The herds in their vastness might have survived—but in 1871 a tannery found that the hides made usable leather, and the incredible slaughter began. Painter J. H. Moser looks over a hunter's shoulder as he guns down bison after bison from a downwind vantage. If he stays low he can kill 100 in a day without spooking the herd, and the skinners in Olaf Seltzer's grim scene will find the carcasses conveniently grouped. For a 150-pound hide, St. Louis dealers quoted three dollars in 1849—a siren song to thousands of hunters, a dirge to millions of bison, gunned to a pitiful few by century's end.

"The Still Hunt" by J. H. Moser, 1888. Opposite: top to bottom, "Held Up" by N. H. Trotter, 1897, and "Hide Hunters" by O. C. Seltzer, n.d.

TOGETHER THEY PROSPERED, TOGETHER THEY PASSED

The skull had come from a fallen buffalo, but herds would amble to it anyway, curious to inspect this anomaly the Indians had reared on the open grassland. The beasts would linger for a rub against the cairn's ragged rocks, milling, grazing, sensing too late the headlong charge of Indian hunters exploding from ambush. The buffalo is amazingly agile—its bones have been found on uplands too rugged for horses—but in a thunderous stampede the horse and hunter usually won the race for life. Cairns may have marked a tribe's hunting grounds—and arrows enforced the claim. Curious bison below hold "An Inquest on the Plains" in A. D. Cooper's arresting canvas of 1890. By then the cairn Karl Bodmer painted in 1833 was keeping futile vigil, searching with hollow eyes for the herds —and the hunters—who would not return.

"An Inquest on the Plains" by A. D. Cooper, 1890. Opposite: "Magic Pile Erected by the Assiniboin Indians" by Karl Bodmer, 1833.

The Frontier Closes

The birds had just wakened and begun to sing that April morning in 1861 when the first shots were fired at Fort Sumter in the harbor at Charleston, South Carolina. Thus the Civil War began. A year later in May of 1862 the Congress in Washington, perhaps celebrating the easy victory at New Orleans after the terrible cost of winning at Shiloh, passed the Homestead Act. President Lincoln signed it, almost routinely. It would become effective January 1, 1863. Then the President and the Congress got on with the harsh problems of the war.

The last week in December, 1862, a Union soldier named Daniel Freeman got a furlough, went home to Nebraska, and borrowed a horse and an ax. Blue overcoat flapping in the bitter wind, Freeman rode 70 miles west from Brownsville, on the Missouri River, cut an armload of stakes, and marked off 160 acres of bottomland on Cub Creek. He returned to Brownsville, persuaded the Register to open the Government Land Office for a few minutes just after midnight on New Year's Day, and filed a homestead claim to the land he had just staked. Then he went back to his regiment.

Daniel Freeman was one of the first of a vast new horde of settlers who under the 1862 law eventually took title to public lands totaling nearly seven times the area of New England. The war dragged on to another April morning three years later when birds were singing outside Appomattox Court House, as men laid down their arms. Then Daniel Freeman went back to Nebraska, proved up on his homestead, and became the sheriff of Gage County.

The first big wave of postwar settlement in 1866 took most of the good land east of the 98th meridian which includes the eastern third of Kansas, Nebraska, and the Dakotas. This was well-watered land with a good deal of timber, and the homesteaders there turned the clock back 200 years, to a way of life the East had outgrown and almost forgotten. They built log cabins, burned wood, cleared fields, drank spring water, ate venison or buffalo steaks, built towns and mills in the river valleys.

But that phase of homesteading soon passed. By the 1870s the frontier had moved on west, to the high plains. That is where the classic traditions of homesteading took shape, the resolute, bearded men and the brave, sunbonneted women living in sod houses on the high, dry, and lonesome land.

The mountain goat, disdained by pioneers for its gamey flavor and by some trophy hunters for its short horns, has maintained its numbers—about 15,000—for centuries. One of the kids' few predators is the golden eagle, which also preys on the pika (above). Another mountain dweller, the ptarmigan (below) grows feather "snowshoes" as its plumage shifts from summer brown to winter white.

Before the first surge of homesteading onto the high plains could begin, however, two problems had to be solved—the buffalo problem and the Indian problem. And crucial to both was the transcontinental railroad.

Surveys for the railroad, before the war began, had made the Indians uneasy. Now as roadbed and rails were pushed westward, the Indians became hostile, and construction crews had to have increasing protection from them. Those crews were being fed buffalo meat and the buffalo, the Indians believed, belonged to them. Here is the account of one meat hunter who worked for the railroad at that time. His name was William F. Cody:

"I started in killing buffalo for the Union Pacific Railroad. I had a wagon with four mules, one driver and two butchers, all brave, well-armed men, myself riding my horse 'Brigham.'

I had to keep a close and careful lookout for Indians before making my run into a herd of buffalo. It was my custom in those days to pick out a herd that seemed to have the fattest cows and young heifers. I would then rush my horse into them, picking out the fattest cows and shooting them down, while my horse would be running alongside of them . . . I have killed from twenty-five to forty buffalo while the herd was circling, and they would all be dropped very close together; that is to say, in a space covering about five acres.

I killed buffalo for the railroad company for twelve months, and during that time the number I brought into camp was kept account of, and at the end of that period I had killed 4,280 buffalo.

During those twelve months I had many fights with the Indians . . . We would make our breastwork around the wheels of the wagon by throwing out the meat, and would protect ourselves by getting behind the buffalo hams. In this manner we held off from forty to sixty Indians on one or two occasions until we received assistance. I would make my smoke signals at once, which the soldiers would instantly see and rush to our rescue. I had five men killed during my connection with the U.P.R.R., three drivers and the others butchers."

Cody, of course, later was known as Buffalo Bill.

Although some 30,000 buffalo still graze on ranch and refuge (left), the closing frontier shattered life for both bison and redskin. Their place in history was recorded with dignity on the 1913 nickel, but was treated as cheap entertainment in traveling Wild West shows (right).

The railroad was completed in 1869 and it simplified the buffalo problem somewhat by cutting the huge main herd of buffalo in two. In the years immediately following, the railroad brought white hunters with modern ammunition, new and more powerful rifles. And the railroad carried back east cargoes of buffalo tongues, buffalo hides, and eventually buffalo bones to be ground up and made into fertilizer.

Although Indians had hunted buffalo for generations, often wastefully, they had done little lasting harm to the herds. More buffalo died then of natural causes—bogged in quicksand, trapped in river ice, victims of blizzards, or pulled down by wolves—than all the Indians could kill. But that was before the white man came with his horse and his gun. Half a century after Lewis and Clark made their epic journey, Dr. F. V. Hayden, a geologist whose surveys for the federal government took him to the upper Missouri country three times between 1853 and 1866, summed up his observations thus:

"As near as I can ascertain, about 250,000 individuals [buffalo] are destroyed every year, about 100,000 being killed for robes . . . The number of males to females [now] seems to be in the ratio of ten to one, and this fact is readily accounted for from the fact that the males are seldom killed when the cows can be obtained . . . besides the robes which are traded to the whites by the Indians, each man, woman, and child requires from one to three robes a year for clothing."

No species can long survive with a ratio of ten males to one female.

Yet as late as 1869 there were still enough buffalo in one herd to keep a Kansas Pacific train immobile for nine hours while they crossed the tracks. And in the early 1870s Texas drovers taking longhorn herds up the Chisholm Trail often had to stop in Oklahoma to let huge herds of buffalo pass ahead of them. In 1871 "skin hunters" began the final systematic slaughter of the southern herd, and from then until 1875 Dodge City, Kansas was the buffalo marketplace of the world. Hides sold for $1.25 each, tongues for 25 cents apiece, and hind quarters for one cent a pound. In 1872 and 1873 the railroads were said to have carried 1,250,000 buffalo hides out of Kansas and nearby territories. Tom Nixon, a

professional hide hunter, killed 120 in 40 minutes, a total of 2,173 from September 15 to October 20. Brick Bond, another professional, killed 250 buffalo in one day and 5,855 in one fall season.

Then the buffalo were gone from the southern plains, and the cattle had arrived.

Back when the Civil War began most of the Texas ranchmen had left their herds to the care of womenfolk and boys, and had taken up the tools of combat. The herds actually were left pretty much to fend for themselves on the open range and in the mesquite thickets. Those herds were Texas longhorns, a half-wild species to begin with, and in the thickets they fought for their lives against bears, cougars, jaguars, and bobcats. They survived and multiplied. When the men came home from the war they were cattle-poor. And the people in New Orleans and St. Louis and Chicago and "back east" were beef-hungry.

In 1866 a few Texans gathered 260,000 head of longhorns and trailed them northward all the way to Sedalia or St. Joseph, Missouri to market. The drovers had trouble with Indians, with flooded rivers, with stampedes. But the next year they drove still more longhorns north, making deals with the Indians or fighting them off, battling weather and floods. By 1867 the railroads were reaching central Kansas and trail herds could be taken to railhead at Abilene and shipped east for the first time.

The next year, 1868, also happened to be the year that James Oliver in South Bend, Indiana made the first chilled-steel plow. That was the plow that could turn the sod of the old buffalo ranges which was far too tough for the old-fashioned plows. Oliver's invention was an omen of wheat farms and dust bowls far off on the horizon. But for now the cattle kept coming out of Texas onto the high plains to fatten on the buffalo grass of western Oklahoma and Kansas and eastern Colorado.

The 1867 purchase of Alaska gave us a new frontier and increased U.S. area by 20 percent. It also added caribou, Dall sheep, musk ox, and polar bear to the nation's wildlife roster; yet in the state seal design above, only the salmon and the seal were included. The walrus opposite, another new species, uses yard-long tusks to help heave its nearly two-ton hulk up onto, and around on, the ice.

Meanwhile, remnants of the northern buffalo herd grazed well up into the Dakotas, Wyoming, and Montana. They were still hunted, but since they were less accessible to markets now, they persisted into the 1880s, as did small pockets of buffalo here and there elsewhere. Before these last open-range buffalo sank closer to extinction, however, a vast new frontier had unexpectedly opened up.

In 1867 Secretary of State Seward purchased Alaska from the Russians for $7,200,000. Critics called it "Seward's Folly," but those who knew Alaska thought we got much the better end of the deal. William Dall, naturalist with an expedition surveying possibilities for telegraph routes for Alaska from 1865 to 1868, wrote an exhaustive report on the area's resources. He saw great potential in salmon, cod, and herring fisheries there, and believed the whaling and the fur trade would be well worth the price paid. He said "the quantity of walrus-tusks annually obtained will average one hundred thousand pounds." And he spoke of the wealth of birds that could be taken for use by milliners.

Charles M. Scammon, captain of Dall's research ship, wrote his own opinion of these matters four years later. He was less optimistic about the walrus and the whale. "Already," he wrote, "the animals have suffered so great a slaughter at their [the whalers] hands that their numbers have been materially diminished . . . making it difficult for the Eskimaux to successfully hunt them."

Starting in 1870 the Alaska Commercial Company, a fur trading establishment which had been awarded a 20-year contract by Congress, exploited sea otters and fur seals much as the Russians had.

In 1881 John Muir, the Scottish-born crusader from California, accompanied E. W. Nelson of the Biological Survey on a trip to Alaska. Later Muir provided this vivid description of walrus hunting:

"A little schooner has a boat out in the edge of the [ice] pack killing walruses, while she is lying a little to the east of the sun. A puff of smoke now and then, a dull report, and a huge animal rears and falls—another, and another, as they lie on the ice without showing any alarm, waiting to be killed, like cattle lying in a barnyard! Nearer, we hear the roar, lion-like, mixed with hoarse grunts, from hundreds of black bundles on the white ice. A small red flag is planted near the pile of slain. Then

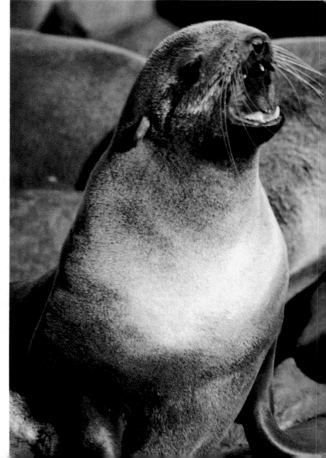

the three men puff off to their schooner, as it is now midnight, and time for the other watch to go to work. . . . These magnificent animals are killed oftentimes for their tusks alone, like buffaloes for their tongues, ostriches for their feathers, or for mere sport and exercise."

Even before the Alaska purchase, explorers and trappers had helped the Eskimos of the northern coast to wipe out the musk ox. The animals of interior Alaska, however, were able to survive the inroads of Eskimos and the white trappers.

Even as the saga of our new northern frontier began to unfold, a fresh chapter was about to be written back on the Great Plains where the dust from the Texas trail herds hung in the air. By 1870 sheepmen with their flocks, regarded as invaders, clashed with the cattlemen in brief but vicious "Wild West" dramas of mingled violence and heroics. At the same time the slow tide of homesteaders edging out across the short-grass plains began to plow and fence the open range. For the next 30 years it was a question of who would survive, the ranchers, the sheepmen, or the homesteaders. They all survived, but the homesteaders with their plows and their barbed wire did put an end, eventually, to open range. They survived by shaping their lives to the demands of the land.

The ranchmen and the sheepmen saw the plains as a land of grass as far as the eye could reach. To the homesteader it was land, fertile land that needed only water to make it as good farmland as a man could find in Iowa or Illinois. A totally different land than his father knew in Iowa or his grandfather back in Ohio or New York State. A land without trees. Where you built a house with walls of sod, that tough-rooted prairie sod laid up, one slab on top of another, self-insulated against winter cold

Fur seals carpet vast rookeries on Alaska's Pribilof Islands in Treasury agent Henry W. Elliott's late 1800s painting above. By 1900 commercial hunters had diminished seal (opposite) and sea otter (left) numbers drastically. Their valuable pelts are composed of a short, very dense and woolly undercoat sprinkled with longer guard hairs. They trap air bubbles which form an insulating layer between bare skin and icy water. Legal protection has stabilized sea otter populations and has made possible government-supervised annual harvests of seals.

and summer heat. A land without brooks, where you dug a well to slake your thirst and to water your livestock. Where you put up a windmill and after the first month you wondered if the wind never stopped blowing. A land of hail and grasshoppers, of drought, of blizzards. A land of extremes.

Here and there the newcomers would find a place where bleached buffalo bones almost covered the grass. A place where hide hunters had made a "surround," got the buffalo to "mill" in a great wheeling movement, and shot them down one by one. Bones that could be gathered by the wagonload and hauled to the railroad maybe 80 miles away, where a buyer for a fertilizer company might pay the hungry homesteader enough money to buy groceries to last his family six months.

In the end the northern herd of buffalo was cut down as the southern herd had been, first by meat hunters, then by hide hunters. And by aristocrats who came out to try their marksmanship, or to get a specially fine robe or head to mount. One small band of buffalo persisted for a time near Lost Park, Colorado, and another—estimated at only 20-odd animals—survived on the upland prairies of Yellowstone Park. The Lost Park herd was destroyed by a group of taxidermists in 1897, but the federal government saved the Yellowstone herd, almost inadvertently, when its grazing area was included in our first national park. There the herd slowly increased in numbers.

Meanwhile public concern for wildlife had been mounting and gathering strength ever since the Civil War. Sportsmen and others who cared about wildlife had been making themselves heard in Washington and in their state capitols. Some of the legislation now seems primitive,

Dauntless migrant of northwestern rivers, Pacific salmon make the dash from sea to freshwater birthplace to mate—then die. Buffeted by rocks and rapids, red sockeye (opposite) turn from silver to vivid red, resting infrequently in placid pools (lower photo) before continuing on. Lewis and Clark first described these unique fish. The silver salmon sketched by Clark (opposite) keeps its color. Dams, siltation, and pollution have severely reduced Pacific salmon, but hatcheries and bypass streams help sustain the beleaguered species.

perhaps, but it shows the way public sentiment was moving—toward conservation. In 1869 Michigan passed the first law protecting passenger pigeons. The same year New York passed a five-year closed season for moose on Long Island. In 1870 California established the first state wildlife refuge in the nation, Lake Merritt, a waterfowl refuge in what is now downtown Oakland.

Then, in 1871, Congress authorized creation of the U.S. Commission on Fish and Fisheries to investigate the condition of food fish in the nation's lakes and coastal waters. And the next year Congress authorized the Commission to introduce or increase salmon, shad, and other valuable food fish, especially in waters under federal control or in interstate and boundary waters. It was also in 1871 that New York established a $30 bounty on wolves in the Adirondacks. And the next year Congress created Yellowstone National Park.

After John Colter's discovery of the hot springs area of Yellowstone around 1808, nearly two decades had passed before two other mountain men, Dave Jackson and Will Sublette, explored the region. They not only verified Colter's seemingly fantastic stories, but added their own accounts of spectacular geysers and boiling mud pots. In 1833 George Catlin, the artist who painted western Indian life in the field, urged a system of national parks to preserve Indian life and culture as well as natural wonders. But the time was not right. In 1870 the Washburn-Langford-Doane expedition was sent to explore the Yellowstone area, and report to Congress. It was their official confirmation of the natural wonders, and mounting public interest in them, which finally moved Congress to act.

The natural wonders of Yellowstone had been saved from private exploitation, but not until Congress passed the Park Protection Act of 1894 was the wildlife there protected from poaching, economic exploitation, and waste. The new law also applied to Yosemite and Sequoia, and would apply to all national parks created thereafter. From then on, both elk and bison herds in the park increased rapidly, and the park authorities began to grapple with the anomaly of pockets of abundance midst a general scarcity of game, a baffling new development which was to confuse conservation attempts throughout the country for several more decades.

Emotional resistance to the idea of allowing some hunting to thin sanctuary herds for their own welfare was one example of the changing public attitude. Though not a constructive one in terms of conservation, it did indicate a significant turn away from the anything-goes market-hunting concepts of the past.

From colonial days, the hunter who took game to sell had been respected and held a position about equivalent to that of the village butcher or the city meat packer today. Haunches of venison, saddles of elk, and braces of birds, from grouse to ducks and geese, hung in the same markets that sold beefsteak, lamb chops, and chickens. This was true through the nineteenth century. Market hunting was a legitimate business, and it had political and economic support in Congress. Among the strongest supporters were the railroads, the eastern tanners, the meat suppliers, and the milliners who used feathers and other bird parts for decoration.

Sportsmen, on the other hand, had fought market hunting for years and had led the public campaign against it. One result was state laws limiting or forbidding it. Arkansas passed the first law banning market hunting of waterfowl in 1875. Two years later Florida passed a law prohibiting the killing of plumed birds or taking eggs from their nests. It was a relatively mild law, but it did mark the beginning of a long fight that culminated in the landmark congressional Lacey Act a quarter of a century later.

In 1878 California and New Hampshire set up game departments chiefly to enforce hunting laws, a step first taken by Massachusetts in 1865. In 1879 Michigan enacted a ten-year closed season on elk. In 1890 Wyoming established a ten-year closed season on buffalo, which was a little like closing the season on saber-tooth cats.

All this conservation activity did not happen as a purely spontaneous public uprising. It was the intensive work of small private groups of influential citizens who sensed what was happening to America's wildlife and who were determined that something be done about it. Here and there were specially eloquent or powerful leaders who were in a position to influence both public opinion and legislation. Among many, two stand out for what they accomplished. One was Theo-

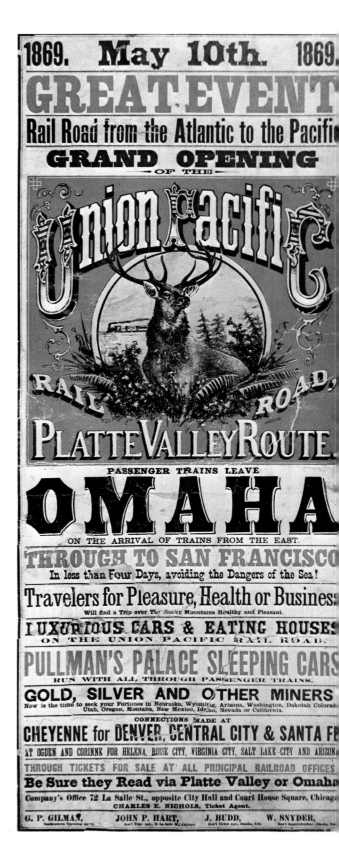

Elk were used to publicize the West to adventurous
Easterners, and new railroads like the Union Pacific sold
firsthand views (opposite). Today elk prosper throughout
western mountain ranges. Early-rising tourists may still
see herds grazing at dawn or hear them bugling in the
autumn rut like the regal bull above. Hunting keeps this
popular game animal in balance with its limited habitat.

dore Roosevelt, the other was George Bird Grinnell.

Theodore Roosevelt went to North Dakota as a young man to regain his health and to live an outdoor life. He was a sportsman-hunter and he became a ranchman. In both capacities he learned a great deal about nature and wildlife, and when he returned east and entered politics it was with a sense of mission about saving the forests and the wildlife of the West. Even before he was elected governor of New York he had gathered a group of kindred spirits and organized the Boone and Crockett Club, one of the first really effective conservation organizations. That was in 1887. It was not a social club, but an action group of sportsmen that included leaders in business, in government, and in public affairs. One of its first goals was the enlargement of Yellowstone National Park and the protection of wildlife there. Virtually every other action taken by the club was also in support of conservation. The Roosevelt viewpoint dominated in those matters, but he had ample backing. And when he became president of the United States he accomplished more than any other president had even attempted in terms of conservation.

George Bird Grinnell was a naturalist and student of Indian life and a co-founder of the Boone and Crockett Club. He was official naturalist with the George Armstrong Custer mission to the Black Hills in 1874, two years before Custer's fatal debacle. In 1875 he was with Capt. William Ludlow of the Army's Corps of Engineers on a reconnaissance expedition in the Yellowstone. From 1880 until 1911 he was editor of *Forest and Stream*, at that time the most influential outdoor publication in the country. Through it he campaigned vigorously for wildlife conservation measures from market-hunting laws and the need for a migratory bird treaty with Canada and Mexico to the creation of Glacier National Park. He was also a founder of the Audubon Society of New York, forerunner of the National Audubon Society.

There were many others vital to the new trend of thinking. They included such gifted, dedicated, and diverse leaders as Gifford Pinchot, John Muir, William T. Hornaday, and Charles Sheldon.

Pinchot was chief of the Bureau of Forestry, forerunner of today's U.S. Forest Service, under Presidents McKinley, Roosevelt, and Taft, but he

8 to 10 years

5 to 6 years

1 year

Driven by curiosity or thirst, shy desert bighorn sheep (top) confront man on occasion. Amazingly agile, most bighorn subspecies are more at home among mountain crags and meadows than in the desert. Come November's mating season, rams square off for usually harmless butting contests. The peculiar skull and horn structure cushions extremely heavy impact during these duels. The horns' rings also reveal the age of the sheep (drawings opposite). Ancient Americans admired bighorns, too; the Inyo Canyon petroglyph above may have reported a kill.

made the whole area of natural resources his field. His philosophy was one of use and renewal. This put him at odds with John Muir who wanted to preserve, to save as wilderness for the most part. Muir to a large degree dominated conservation in the Far West; he was a leader in creating a 4,000,000-acre Sierra Forest Reserve in 1891 and in establishing Yosemite and Sequoia National Parks. In 1892 he organized the Sierra Club.

Pinchot dominated forest conservation at the federal level, however, and under his management and with Theodore Roosevelt's backing, national forests were established on the basis of use, with 148,000,000 acres set aside between 1901 and 1909. Together the efforts of Roosevelt, Pinchot, and Muir secured for wildlife millions of acres of habitat and started a trend toward reserving still more.

Hornaday was a naturalist and conservationist whose first concern was for the vanishing buffalo. In 1886 he led a scientific expedition that took inventory and found approximately 540 surviving buffalo in the entire United States, most of them in the rejuvenated Yellowstone Park herd or in zoos or on private lands. Hornaday helped form the American Bison Society which campaigned successfully for the first two national bison reserves; they were established in the Wichita Mountains of Oklahoma in 1907 and in the Flathead Valley of Montana in 1909. The Society raised money to buy buffalo to stock the new reserves, some animals were transferred from the Yellowstone herd, and some were given by the New York Zoological Park of which Hornaday was then director. There they have thrived and multiplied. Small herds have since been stocked on several other Canadian and American reserves. Commercial production of buffalo is also increasing.

Charles Sheldon, another member of the Boone and Crockett Club, became so fascinated with the desert bighorn sheep while on a hunting trip to Mexico in 1898 that he spent the rest of his life learning more about it. From the age of 36, he made a series of studies of all the races of American wild sheep. To learn their distribution, habits, and racial characteristics, he pursued them along America's rocky backbone from Mexico to Alaska, living as close to them as the wary creatures would allow. He was often alone for weeks at a time and he became almost as adept as the sheep at negotiating rocky ledges and crevasses.

In Alaska the lure of unmapped wilderness drew Sheldon to Mount McKinley. The sheer beauty of the 20,300-foot giant of a mountain so captivated the man that he led the 11-year fight which made it a national park in 1917. But Sheldon is best remembered for his dedication to scientific knowledge, without which he knew wise decisions about wildlife could not be made.

Until concern over diminishing herds of all kinds reached Congress, wildlife, particularly in the West, had been assumed to be an unlimited natural resource. Everywhere travelers went, bison, deer, elk, and antelope were killed as a matter of course, whether for a trailside meal cooked over a campfire or for a good dinner in the best hotel around. Market hunters took by far the greatest toll, but there were other heavy users.

Wild game was the only food for most of the 10,000 persons who streamed into the Black Hills looking for gold in the 1850s. Elk were so nearly exterminated in South Dakota that eventually they had to be restocked from Wyoming. During the last quarter of the nineteenth century approximately 30,000 black bears were killed annually for their skins, a staggering total of 750,000. By 1910 relatively few bears remained alive outside the protection of national parks in the Rockies, Cascades, and the Sierra Nevada. From 1870 until 1900 a part of the Great Plains in eastern Dakota was called chicken country because hunters there shipped barrel after barrel of prairie chickens to markets in the East. No exact figures are known, but millions of the birds were killed.

Scattered local laws were enacted to check all this slaughter, but they were only moderately effective. In 1878 Iowa adopted a bag limit of 25 prairie chickens and other game birds per day, the first bag-limit law in the country. In 1876 Wisconsin was first to ban the use of dogs in hunting deer, and five years

The market hunters' heyday saw many species go for fashion and feast. Sometimes a whole mockingbird was stuffed to perch on a modish hat (right); also used were the breast feathers of the grebe (opposite). Ice box cars (center) facilitated shipping; their contents brought a good price on eastern markets, witness the shipping list above.

120

J. C. JACKSON
WHOLESALERS
POULTRY AND WILDFOWL
BALT. MD. EST. 1786

NAME	SHIPPING PRICES	PRICE/PAIR
Buffell Head		$.30 –.50
Brant		1.25
Black Duck		1.25
Whistler		.30 .50
Butterballs		1.00
Broad Bills		.30 .50
Goose		2.00
Red Heads		2.50
Canvas Back Prime		5.00 – 7.00
" " Regular		2.00 – 5.00
Old Sausaw		.70 .90
Ruddy		.90 – 1.00
Coot (Scoter)		.50
Sprigtail		.50
Widgeon		.50

later Michigan had outlawed the use of traps, snares, and pitfalls for taking deer; but it was not until 1895 that Michigan limited each hunter to five deer a season. By then other states had begun limiting open seasons, but wildlife populations continued to drop alarmingly.

By the late 1890s the situation was recognized as a national problem requiring federal action. Various remedies were proposed and discussed by conservation organizations; finally Iowa Congressman John F. Lacey, a Boone and Crockett Club member and friend of Theodore Roosevelt, proposed an act to prohibit virtually all interstate shipment of game which had been taken in violation of state law. His proposal gathered support and was passed by both the House and the Senate in May of 1900. President McKinley signed it at once.

The Lacey Act was one of the most important actions ever taken to preserve and protect American wildlife. It put the market hunter out of business whether he dealt in birds for their plumage, eggs, or flesh, or in mammals for their meat, pelts, even their antlers. It also made illegal the importation of foreign wildlife except by special permit from the Secretary of Agriculture. By vesting administration of the Act in the U.S. Biological Survey, the new law raised that almost forgotten agency from taxonomic biology, rodent control, and bird study to a position of real power. From this firm base, today's Fish and Wildlife Service was created.

Ten years earlier, in 1890, the U.S. Census Bureau had reported that it could no longer pinpoint the frontier in the United States. That, of course, could mean that there no longer was a frontier. It could also mean the frontier was diffused, scattered all over the West. Or it could mean that there were differing definitions of the word "frontier." Whatever meaning one chose, the Census Bureau's announcement conveyed the idea that a basic change had occurred that would profoundly affect the land, the wildlife, even the lives and outlook of the people. In other words, an environmental evolution—perhaps even revolution—was bringing us inexorably into a new ecological age.

Yet the whole panorama of western wildlife— herds of elk moving up the mountain slopes to summer range in springtime and coming down to the valleys in the fall, the scream of a mountain lion at night, the fearful glimpse of a grizzly by day, herds of pronghorn and deer, even an occasional buffalo—was still a very visible part of the frontier which the Census Bureau now said had vanished. Sod houses were still being built and range wars still flared around the water holes. The frontier didn't vanish with the last long drive of Texas longhorns or the last acre of open range in the big-ranch country. As late as 1920 frontier conditions persisted in the Great Basin between the Rockies and the Sierra Nevada.

Nevertheless, change *had* come about with startling swiftness and awesome breadth after the first transcontinental railroad brought the vast expanses of the Old West within the reach of every adventurous spirit. Pioneering was soon going to be a memory for most of the people. Already it was a legend for virtually everyone east of the Mississippi.

By 1900 it was also clear that we had actually wiped out some species of wildlife and that others were in danger. Already it was plain to those who grasped the web-of-life concept of nature that the loss of any species made us all somewhat poorer. It was one of the new ways of thinking now shaping up, new ways of looking at our natural environment. The examples of the passenger pigeon and the buffalo were there for anyone to see. The tide of public opinion was turning. A broad movement toward conservation of our natural resources, particularly of wildlife, timber, and water, had begun.

But the turn of the century brought new and unanticipated problems for wildlife. We had invented the automobile which soon would call for—and get—highways to every corner of the continent, highways that would spread concrete and macadam over millions of acres of wildlife habitat and create execution lanes for countless numbers of the wildlife community, from skunks and slow-moving opossums to deer. We had invented the airplane which would invade wildlife's last retreats from civilization. The airplane too would call for and get more millions of acres for take-off and landing fields. Conservationists now saw that they must lead the way toward far more sweeping reforms of nineteenth century practices. In this twentieth century, we would have to learn new lessons and apply new rules. We had arrived at a whole new frontier.

ISLANDS
OF WILDNESS

Land free for the taking! Timber, gold, grass for the fattening herd . . . rich
bottomlands awaiting the seed. Generations rolled westward to claim it, crowding out
elk and antelope, bear and bison. But settlers, railroad crews, and survey parties
like the one Albert Bierstadt portrayed in 1859 bypassed the continent's
innermost sanctuaries. There, where geysers erupted and waterfalls cascaded, remnant
herds roamed undisturbed. In these havens they endured until conservation-minded
Americans made parks out of their last retreats—and thus helped assure their survival.

"Minerva Terrace" by Thomas Moran, 1872. Opposite: left to right, detail from "Catching and Cooking Fish without Removing Them from the Hook" by William H. Holmes, 1872, and "Tower Falls" by John H. Renshawe, 1883.

YELLOWSTONE: A SPECTACULAR BEGINNING

*Should each man stake a land claim? The question hung
in the smoke of a Yellowstone campfire one night in 1870.
A band of Montanans had explored this playground of
ancient volcanoes and retreat for lordly elk. They had
seen sights like Tower Falls, its thunder almost audible in
John H. Renshawe's painting of 1883, and thermal pools
by a fish-filled lake, where in 1872 William H. Holmes
portrayed anglers catching and cooking with one sweep of
the rod. Who should own this magnificence? Everyone,
suggested Cornelius Hedges. In 1872 Congress gazed at
wonders painted by Thomas Moran, and made of
Yellowstone the world's first national park. Here elk and
bison survived civilization's tide. Now they thrive on
federal big game refuges and throughout the West.*

"Yosemite Valley" by Thomas Hill, 1889. Opposite: "Yosemite Fountain on the Southwest Side of the Cathedral Spur, near Mt. Lyell"
by John Muir, n.d., and photograph of John Muir.

YOSEMITE: VALLEY OF VANQUISHED GRIZZLIES

*Uzumati, they called themselves, "the Grizzlies."
They were a small Indian clan living in a sculptured
Sierra valley, and their name stuck to the land: Uzumati
—Yosemite. No grizzlies survive there today, but the
little creatures thrive. "A hot spark of life . . . a small
nugget of mountain vigor and valor," wrote John Muir
of the Douglas squirrel. The Scottish-born naturalist
delighted too in the companionship of golden-mantled
ground squirrel, jackrabbit, mountain quail, and water
ouzel. Muir's sketches of sights such as Yosemite
Fountain, his descriptions which matched the grandeur
of Thomas Hill's colorful painting of
1889, and his ceaseless struggle with
thoughtless logger and stockman
helped get nearly a million acres
set aside in 1890 as Yosemite,
Sequoia, and General Grant
National Parks.*

"Island in Princess Louisa Inlet, B.C." by Albert Bierstadt, ca. 1880. Opposite: photograph of Theodore Roosevelt.

WASHINGTON ISLANDS: A PLACE FOR PUFFINS

Early parks were for people, havens from the harried humdrum of lives pledged to progress. But progress imperiled wildlife, too. As coastal cities grew, tiny seabird rookeries became arenas for rival egg and plume sellers squabbling over raiding rights. Finally an idea was born: refuges for animals, where man enters under strict rules or stays away entirely. The idea had a tough ally: President Theodore Roosevelt. In 1903 he created the first national wildlife refuge on Pelican Island, Florida; in the next six years he added 31 more. Islets like this one which Albert Bierstadt painted in British Columbia about 1880 resemble the more southerly Washington Islands refuges established in 1907. Here the puffin parades its harlequin beak and nests among 13 other species of seabirds. Soon there were mainland ranges for bison, elk, pronghorn, musk ox, bighorn sheep; next came waterfowl refuges, sprawling wetlands where migrants splash down by the thousands. In each, the benefits radiate to the far edges of the web of life.

GRAND CANYON: LIVING LABORATORY

Around 1540 Coronado's conquistadors gazed into awesome Grand Canyon and called it "a useless piece of country." Three centuries later, men found all too many uses for this high plateau, cloven as if by the wrath of gods. Trappers sought pelts, railroad men plotted routes, prospectors panned for nuggets. Then came John Wesley Powell. The Civil War took his arm but not his nerve; in 1869 he led a survey party through the abyss by boat. Today millions visit this national park, seeing mighty monoliths like Shivas Temple (opposite) as Thomas Moran saw it in 1892. But few know the canyon as Powell did, a mile deep in its heart, riding the Colorado River through months of struggle and solitude. His discoveries helped make the area a national monument in 1908, and in 1919 it became a national park. All but lost in H. H. Nichols' engraving, three mule deer roam the North Rim's Kaibab Plateau, harsh classroom for wildlife scientists in the 1920s, and sole home of one of our showiest tree-dwelling mammals, the tuft-eared and graceful Kaibab squirrel.

"The High Plateaus" by H. H. Nichols, n.d.; above, photograph of John Wesley Powell and Tau-qu, a Paiute chief, by J. K. Hillers, 1872. Opposite: "Shivas Temple" by Thomas Moran, 1892.

"Toltec Gorge, Colorado" by Thomas Moran, 1892. Opposite: top to bottom, "Thunderstorm in the Rocky Mountains" by Albert Bierstadt, 1859, and photograph of Enos Mills (hatless) and official party at the dedication of Rocky Mountain National Park, 1915.

THE ROCKIES: A MAN TO MATCH THE MOUNTAINS

At the dedication of his beloved Rocky Mountain National Park in 1915, Enos Mills alone posed without a hat. A small thing—yet it symbolized the spirit of this lone writer-naturalist who had lectured, campaigned, written hundreds of articles, and buttonholed congressmen until his mountains were safe. Mills was a living legend, a mountaineer who probed alpine crannies like Toltec Gorge (left) where Thomas Moran painted in 1892. He knew the spent fury Albert Bierstadt tried to capture in his 1859 oil of a passing Rockies storm . . . knew, too, the Rocky Mountain bighorn sheep that found footholds where not even Mills dared venture. Thousands now glimpse the bighorn, living symbol of the park that protects it.

"A View of Karakakooa, in Owyhee" by J. W. Webber and W. Byrne, n.d. Opposite: "Volcano of Kaluea Pele" by Titian R. Peale, 1840.

HAWAII VOLCANOES: BORN IN FIRE, KEPT IN PEACE

Migrating birds blown off course . . . seeds borne in by wind or wave . . . small animals washed ashore on flotsam—it is fascinating to speculate how life colonized the once-barren volcanic upthrusts of the Hawaiian Islands. Polynesian seafarers who peopled the empty isles 2,000 years ago introduced the now-wild pig, and perhaps unwittingly the rat. Their descendants in 1778 paddled out with gifts for Captain Cook who left with them the goat. But what of the only native mammal, the Hawaiian bat? Could it have crossed the sea? We only know that here, on today's deforested slopes in Hawaii Volcanoes National Park, which Titian Peale painted in 1840 while accompanying the Wilkes Expedition, the tiny ogre roosts in scattered trees like the candlenut. Farther out is Hawaiian Islands National Wildlife Refuge, nearly 2,000 acres of islets sprinkling 1,000 miles of ocean. There rare birds once sought by milliners live secure—far-flung proof of the American people's commitment to sanctuary for wildlife.

The Tide
Turns

By the end of World War I, Americans recognized that we had left behind our youthful time of overwhelming plenty, in terms of wildlife and wilderness, and that we faced a future of growing scarcities and threats to what remained. But the broad, popular movement toward conservation was still more an emotional cause than a controlled science. Indeed, we still failed to recognize many basic laws of nature, so we were forced to discover them the hard way.

A classic case of how we lurched ahead toward sensible conservation through trial and error may be seen in what happened to the deer on the Kaibab Plateau. This is a beautiful stretch of national forest land in Arizona some 8,000 feet above sea level, surrounded on three sides by mile-deep canyons (Grand Canyon to the south, Kanab Creek to the west, Marble Canyon to the east). It is a place of peaceful repose; the Indian name, Kaibab, means "mountain lying down" as if in sleep. It also seemed to the Indians a place of plentiful deer: another name means "Buckskin Mountain."

Originally the plateau had a herd of about 3,000 mule deer, for which there was ample forage in the more than 1,000,000 acres of open woodland interspersed with mountain meadows. Paiutes and Navajos came to the plateau to collect piñon nuts and vegetables and to hunt the deer.

It drew white settlers and hunters too—ranchers who began to graze cattle and sheep in the late 1800s and sportsmen who came looking for big game trophies. The sportsmen and other visitors were increasingly disturbed, however, by the excessive numbers of deer that were being taken. In 1906, in response to a nationwide campaign to save the animals, President Theodore Roosevelt set the Kaibab area aside as the Grand Canyon National Game Preserve.

He also ordered a predator control program to protect the deer by eliminating their nonhuman enemies. Between 1906 and 1923 it was estimated that Forest Service employees killed 674 cougars, 11 wolves, 3,000 coyotes, and 120 bobcats on the Kaibab. Roosevelt himself came in 1913 with his sons Archie and Quentin and his nephew Nicholas, and led them on predator hunts.

The deer problem was complicated by the ranchers who had succeeded by 1906 in packing the plateau with 20,000 sheep and 9,000 cattle, to the point that overgrazing had damaged the range. When told to take their animals elsewhere in deference to the deer, not all the ranchers complied; thousands of sheep and cattle remained to compete with the natural wildlife. Yet the major problem lay not with the livestock nor with the banished predators and hunters, but with the deer themselves—specifically, their rapid rate of reproduction. By 1918 the deer numbered close to 40,000. By 1924 their population had exploded beyond the 100,000 mark. In that winter of 1924 an estimated 60,000 deer died at Kaibab, weakened by starvation and a series of storms. Forced to act, the Forest Service reversed game preserve policy and issued special hunting licenses. But even this measure failed to alleviate the problem.

Wild West novelist Zane Grey and other enthusiasts developed the idea that the overpopulation could be dramatically reduced by driving large numbers of deer down and across the Grand Canyon to other deer-depleted parts of Arizona. Gathering in the common cause, cowboys and Indians equipped with cowbells and clanging pots and pans formed a line to sweep the woodland. But they tripped over another then-unknown law of nature: deer browse in a circular direction within a radius of a few miles. Beyond that distance they refuse to be driven, will even get down on their knees and try to crawl back through the human chain of beaters to "home base." A thunderstorm further confounded the roundup. Not one deer reached the canyon's far rim where a prize of $2.50 for each delivered deer had awaited any lucky drover.

So the population explosion continued. The plateau was completely denuded of its grasses; no aspen or juniper tree could reproduce; spruce and fir trees, as high as the deer could reach, were nibbled to the trunk. Tens of thousands of emaciated deer died. Forest Service managers desperately sought to open up the plateau to hunters, but well-

Our national symbol the bald eagle gained a new identity in World War I, appearing on posters to make the ultimate appeal to Americans—one more patriotic effort, whether in war bonds or manpower, for democracy. Ironically, the same was being asked of the Germans by another bird of prey, the Kaiser's golden eagle.

meaning opponents throughout the nation balked; apparently they preferred to let starvation do its work slowly and cruelly. The governor of Arizona threatened to call out the National Guard to prevent Forest Service employees from carrying out the needed reduction.

Finally, by 1930, wiser heads prevailed and regulated hunting of deer was permitted while natural predators were allowed to return. Thus the number of deer was reduced to 20,000. Since then careful control has brought the herd down to about 10,000, one for each 100 of Kaibab's acres. Despite a recurrence of deer overpopulation in the 1950s which again damaged the range, the once-beautiful plateau is at long last regaining some of its verdant charm. Nevertheless, a visitor, seeing the "skirted" trees which have still not totally recovered from the depredation, has the sense of walking through an historic battleground.

The Kaibab deer crisis probably was the turning point in our national approach to wildlife problems. Studying what had happened there, serious Americans began to see how ignorant we still were about nature and how urgent was the need for a whole new profession: overall wildlife management based on fundamental research. But even as early managers tried to apply new knowledge (concentrating first on big game, then smaller game, wildfowl, and fish), mistakes—costly mistakes—continued to be made.

Yellowstone Park was another example of how difficult it was for us to learn from our own history. By 1911 officials saw that the northern Yellowstone herd which always wintered inside the park had mushroomed in size. Park officials began live-trapping elk and shipping them to zoos and unoccupied ranges, but this market was soon glutted. As the nearby town of Jackson Hole, Wyoming

Skyrocketing populations of mule deer in the 1920s greatly damaged vegetation (opposite left) on Arizona's Kaibab Plateau. Various methods of control were tried, including the use of government hunters (opposite above) to reduce the herds. These measures were successful for a time but the Kaibab saw another great population crisis 30 years later; damage done then is slowly healing (left) and the deer (above) are once again in prime condition.

141

grew, the elk were increasingly hindered from migrating to winter range at lower elevations. A national elk refuge was established near the park about 1913, but that was only a temporary solution. By the 1930s the problem was serious. Range was deteriorating, the herd was still expanding rapidly, and the elk were in trouble from disease as well as starvation. To control the size of the herds and keep them in balance with the food supplies, the Park Service and the Montana Game Commission endorsed a hunting season within the park. The resulting national outcry was the Kaibab story all over again. But scientific sanity prevailed and by 1943 controlled hunting had reduced the elk herds by about one half, back to within the carrying capacity of the land.

The elk problem remains controversial because mounting pressures from tourism, recreation, and real estate development continue to limit the elks' range. Annual reductions of the herds are still necessary despite opposition to killing elk, or what might be called the "Bambi complex."

Reruns of the Kaibab deer and Yellowstone elk dramas have occurred repeatedly in other local and state situations. It happened with deer in Pennsylvania. It happened with the Dall sheep in Mount McKinley National Park. It happened with the moose on Isle Royale in Lake Superior. The solution, in almost every case, has been reduction of the herds by restoration of predators or by hunting, until the range could support the animals again.

Attempts to eradicate bothersome species too may backfire as beneficial animals are also accidently destroyed. With predators absent, rodents and insects multiply unchecked, and man may find that his meddling has caused more harm than good.

Man has, of course, been blindly upsetting nature's balances in too many ways for too many years. As our technology has grown and our population increased with all its demands for living space, we have multiplied the effects of these changes on wildlife habitat.

The Welland Canal offers yet another example of the freakish kind of thing that happens when man, ignoring wildlife and ecology, plunges arrogantly ahead on his own. In building the canal in 1829 to bypass Niagara Falls from Lake Ontario to Lake Erie, the way was opened for sea lampreys and alewives to reach farther inland than ever before. The 16-inch lamprey, an eel-like parasite that fastens itself to a healthy fish and sucks out its vital juices, had established itself in Lake Erie by the 1920s. The lake trout was its favorite victim. From Erie it went all the way to Lake Superior by the 1950s and virtually wiped out the trout before researchers found a chemical that is toxic to lamprey larvae but harmless to other fish and to plants.

The alewives, small fish of the herring family, invaded the Great Lakes through the canal in the 1930s. Because the lampreys had killed most of their predators, the alewives multiplied at an astonishing rate, crowding out more desirable native fish. Today the alewife population seems to be declining, largely as a consequence of planting coho salmon and chinook salmon in the lakes every year since 1964. The salmon not only eat the alewives but provide new and excellent sport fishing. There is always a risk in introducing an alien species into any environment, but the salmon, in this instance, apparently have been helpful on all counts.

STANDING	FLYING	ON THE WATER
Divers		
Upright stance. Feet near back. Large feet.	*Short thick body. Short wings, tail. Feet behind tail.*	*Set low. Tail touching water.*
Surface feeders		
Horizontal stance. Feet near center. Small feet.	*Longer body. Long wings, tail. Feet under tail.*	*Set high. Tail, wings high. Tail at angle.*

Wetlands are primary among our precious resources, yet they are being lost to agricultural drainage and commercial landfills. Each year less waterfowl habitat remains in the Midwest's pothole country, known as the "duck factory." Mallards often nest at water's edge (opposite below); unlike diving ducks, these surface-feeders glean tender roots from "bottoms-up" feeding in shallow water.

Such unpredictable wildlife crises and emergency solutions did not make for a sensible U.S. conservation policy. Intelligent stewardship of wildlife, that priceless national asset, would not be possible until a new breed of American philosopher-scientists emerged. These new leaders, like Thoreau in the nineteenth century, would have to assert themselves over the technologists and traditionalists of their day before trial-and-error approaches would be abandoned.

Aldo Leopold was the man who first analyzed American wildlife's basic problems correctly and worked out the fundamentals of game management. Leopold was a forester, a naturalist, a philosopher, and an educator. Fortunately he was also a writer who could say things clearly and memorably. Recognizing from the Kaibab and Yellowstone fiascos that prohibiting all hunting on big, federally-held areas actually aggravated species' survival problems, he presented a paper in 1920 advocating the establishment of numerous small, temporary refuges in the national forests. These refuges would have to be maintained by trained and decisive managers who would respond sensitively to the life signals of the animals. Obviously the success of such a program would depend on (in his words) "non-political game departments with complete flexibility of administration."

In 1925, in an article in the *Bulletin* of the American Game Protective Association, Leopold first stated his theory of game management. The key words were "environment" and "cropping." Basically the system, or science, was built around the problem of keeping shifting numbers of wildlife balanced with their changing supplies of food and cover. This called for knowledge of the life patterns of wildlife—patterns such as the relationship between alewives and salmon. The need to acquire that knowledge has led us from such vigils as that of Charles Sheldon stalking the bighorn, to tagging and banding of birds and other animals, and to today's radio tracking of transistorized animals. With information collected in these new ways and with computers to digest the data, wildlife scientists now are able to forecast the effect of almost any measure proposed to limit or to extend a wildlife species in any given area.

Leopold's theories stood the test of practical application and answered questions that had plagued conservationists for years. He expanded those theories when he was asked to present a series of lectures on game management at the University of Wisconsin in 1929. This led to his book *Game Management* which is still a basic text in the field. It also led to his years as professor of wildlife management at the University of Wisconsin. He died at the age of 61 while helping a neighbor fight a grass fire. His death was a severe blow to conservation, but besides his game management text he left *A Sand County Almanac*, one of the most readable, most ecologically important books in print.

The early applications of wildlife management and conservation centered on waterfowl. In the 1920s the duck flights up and down the major inland flyways began to decline. The number of duck hunters was steadily increasing. The combination spelled trouble. What had happened was that in the postwar surge of agriculture, when the United States was asked to feed the world, wetlands were drained and put into cultivation. This deprived ducks and geese of nesting grounds and winter refuges. To stop these losses, the idea of setting aside waterfowl refuges was proposed. This movement got started in 1924 with the passage of the Upper Mississippi River Wildlife and Fish Refuge Act. It authorized only $1,000,000 for waterfowl refuges, but in 1929

Persistent drought and high winds conspired to create the 1930s dust bowl. No roots held the light soil and farms were abandoned throughout the plains (opposite above). Wildlife, especially waterfowl (above), fared the worst. Farmers (opposite below) are wiser now, selecting seed adapted to changing weather patterns, planting crops perpendicular to prevailing winds, and putting in "shelter belts"—rows of trees to break the relentless winds.

144

the Norbeck-Andresen Migratory Bird Conservation Act increased federal appropriations for this purpose.

New troubles came with the dust storms of the 1930s. A drought cycle struck, fields that had been stripped of native grass in the rush to grow wheat were abandoned, and the soil began to blow away. Week after week, month after month, the dust blew. Black blizzards stormed across the plains, the gritty clouds sometimes going all the way to the East Coast, until the dry cycle eased away. Then the grass slowly began to heal the scarred earth, skies were blue again, and waterfowl flights to and from nesting grounds, which had decreased sharply during the dust, grew in numbers.

In 1934 Congress passed the Duck Stamp Act, a measure which sportsmen had proposed and fought for. It required all waterfowl hunters to buy a special stamp, the proceeds of which were used solely to restore the ravaged waterfowl breeding grounds and refuges. The stamps cost one dollar in the beginning, a fee gradually increased to five dollars, and between 1934 and 1974 duck stamp receipts totaled more than $150,000,000. The refuges which that money has bought, and now supports, have become a part of the National Wildlife Refuge System. The success of the Duck Stamp Act demonstrated the willingness of sportsmen to tax themselves for the privilege of hunting, and to maintain wildlife populations. The program it financed has been immensely important not only for ducks and geese but also for all nongame birds and other animals that thrive in a wetland environment.

Fishermen too had their troubles. After World War I there were more fishermen and, seemingly, fewer fish. In 1926 they asked for, and Congress passed, legislation ending commercial fishing for game fish such as black bass. In 1930 the Institute

The canvasback (opposite), esteemed as a prime table bird, has had to face the battle against pollution and disappearing nesting habitat in the past century. Work to save this diving duck is financed with revenue from waterfowl hunters' licenses, called duck stamps (above).

for Fisheries Research was organized at the University of Michigan under Carl L. Hubbs. Adopting the tenets of Aldo Leopold, the institute focused on the problems of improving fish habitat. Pollution of lakes and streams demanded attention. By the early 1930s the Izaak Walton League of America was leading that crusade, but it took until 1948 to get even a temporary federal law controlling water pollution. This was extended in 1956 and now is backed by the stronger Water Quality Act of 1965 and subsequent legislation of the 1960s and 1970s. Nationwide restoration of fish resources had to wait for the Dingell-Johnson Act of 1950 which earmarked a ten percent excise tax on fishing gear for that purpose.

When Franklin D. Roosevelt took office as president in 1933 many conservationists had high hopes for new initiatives in wildlife conservation. They were not disappointed. In his effort to solve Depression problems, various public projects were launched, the T.V.A. and the C.C.C. getting under way in 1933, followed by the S.C.S. in 1935. They were to repair the land, enhance and preserve natural habitats, and provide work, all at the same time.

The Tennessee Valley Authority was hailed all over the world as a practical demonstration of complete watershed planning that revitalized an impoverished area, stopped disastrous flooding, and provided vast quantities of electricity as well as improving waterways.

The Civilian Conservation Corps was manned primarily by unemployed youths from the cities who had everything to learn about the outdoors. Yet they built roads in the national forest, repaired small dams, solved erosion problems in parks and forests, replanted trees, and built needed facilities. The Soil Conservation Service literally changed the face of America's farmland as it tackled the never-ending problem of soil erosion.

One of the best things Roosevelt did for conservation was to name J. N. "Ding" Darling Chief of the Bureau of Biological Survey in 1934. Darling was a nationally known conservationist as well as a Pulitzer Prize-winning cartoonist from Iowa. Among

the accomplishments which may have led to his presidential appointment was the system of fish and wildlife education which he had helped to set up (and even helped personally to finance) at the University of Iowa. Its purpose was to train urgently needed professional conservationists. Darling brought this timely idea to Washington where he launched a similar but much more ambitious program in 1935.

It was called the Cooperative Wildlife Research Unit Program and it enabled ten land grant colleges to begin training thousands of young men for professional careers in wildlife work. The program combined field research with classroom training. The costs were shared by the colleges, the state conservation departments, and the American Wildlife Institute, a nonprofit association of industries, other groups, and individuals.

Darling was responsible for the first North American Wildlife Conference, called by President Roosevelt in 1936. It assembled biologists, administrators, and sportsmen to discuss wildlife problems. He also was responsible for the establishment in 1936 of the National Wildlife Federation to coordinate the activities of local and state conservation groups. He was its first president.

The Roosevelt years were a time of intense activity. Conservation issues were getting more attention than ever before. By the time the first young wildlife graduates received their diplomas, Congress had passed another landmark conservation bill which would put them all to work. The Federal Aid in Wildlife Restoration Act of 1937, better known as the Pittman-Robertson Act, earmarked a ten percent excise tax on sporting arms and ammunition to be used in wildlife projects throughout the country. Its provisions had far-reaching effects in upgrading state fish and game departments from primarily law enforcement units, often limited by partisan politics, to professional staffs of qualified specialists.

It was an encouraging time. Scientists, lay organizations, government, and industry were learning to pool resources and to coordinate attacks on our nationwide wildlife problems. Then the dark clouds of World War II boiled up over Europe and broke with a blinding flash at Pearl Harbor.

War years are not a good time for man or beast. As we had learned between 1914 and 1918, they are wasted years when respect for life, any form of life, is diminished. The years 1941 to 1945 were no exception. As wildlife professionals went into military training, refuge lands and fisheries had to be neglected. The establishment of expansive military bases with their Quonset huts, artillery ranges, airports, and miles of roads and fencing preempted land which was formerly wildlife habitat. Military maneuvers conducted by the tank corps chewed up acres of desert and seashore. Seabirds and shellfish suffered the effects of huge oil slicks from torpedoed tankers.

NOBODY'S CONSTITUENTS.

Conservation money was scarce in 1937, but Ding Darling (opposite on left with Aldo Leopold) campaigned with his no-nonsense cartoons (above). Congress has answered these early nudges with laws that tax sporting gear; the 1950 Dingell-Johnson Act is one. Thus, fishermen like those on the Yellowstone River (opposite) help pay to restore the resource they use.

After Rachel Carson's Silent Spring *appeared in 1962,*
an awakened public took a long, hard look at indiscrimi-
nate pesticide use. Sprayed from planes and helicopters
(above), then carried to earth by wind and water, biolo-

But not all of the war's deleterious effects on wildlife were as clearly perceived as these, nor did they all end when the shooting stopped. One was a new pesticide called dichlorodiphenyl-trichloroethane which had been patented in Switzerland in the late 1930s. It was so effective that its discoverer Paul Müller was awarded a Nobel Prize. The chemical's name was shortened to DDT and in World War II our health units found it amazingly effective for killing fleas, lice, mosquitoes, and a host of other insect pests, thus controlling malaria, typhus, and other diseases. After the war DDT and a number of other chlorinated hydrocarbons were widely used in the United States and abroad by public health workers, by farmers, and by householders.

A number of environmentalists raised questions about these new pesticides. They seemed to be bad for birds, fishes, and other small animals. But the new chemical was touted as the answer to all insect problems and was sold in steadily increasing amounts until 1962 when Rachel Carson's book *Silent Spring* was published. Miss Carson indicted the whole DDT family, cited chapter and verse, gave evidence of serious damage to wildlife, and possible threats to human health.

The chemical industry rose in wrath at Miss Carson and her book, but President Kennedy's prestigious Science Advisory Committee studied the matter and issued a detailed report recommending that all registered uses of persistent toxic pesticides be canceled. Not until 1972, however, did the newly constituted Environmental Protection Agency in Washington finally forbid the use of DDT in the United States except in special cases and with special permission. But by then, the chemical, whose life span may run to ten years, had accumulated in soil, insects, birds, fish, and even mammals.

Where DDT was used in large quantities, birds which ate DDT-loaded earthworms died in spasm. Laboratory tests showed that the chemical could cause brain and liver damage and, particularly in birds, severely affect reproduction. In fact, egg

gists fear that these poisons enter every link of the food chain. Among other ill effects, birds like the roseate tern laid eggs (right) with shells so thin that they broke during incubation; some laid eggs with no shells at all.

shells of some species of birds became so thin as a result of DDT use that they broke before they could be hatched. The chemical spread all over the earth and was even found in snow, ice, and fish in the Antarctic. Pacific Coast seals aborted from it, or bore sickly pups. Studies have found that even humans living near the sites of heavy DDT use had poisons in their fatty tissue and in mothers' milk.

Despite its extensive use, DDT never succeeded in eliminating any species of insect. On the contrary, some insect targets of DDT soon evolved resistant strains. Evidence suggests that the birds, fish, and mammals, with their longer life spans, would do so much more slowly.

Today we have evolved into a nation that recognizes the necessity of environmental conservation. We may not all agree on how it can be achieved, but we know that natural balances are vital. We know that any environment lacking wildlife is out of balance and may even be a signal that we, ourselves, are becoming a threatened species. Since passage of the 1966 Endangered Species Preservation Act, we keep an official list of endangered wildlife species and seek means of saving them. [For a current list by states, see Appendix—Ed.]

We admit that human beings and their culture have had and in the future will continue to have an impact on wildlife, in many instances an unfortunate and even disastrous impact. Some species of animals have proved they can adapt to life with man, but others totally lack this adaptive ability. For those, there must be sanctuaries, special reserved areas. We have set up a number of such refuges where at least sample populations can be protected. The grizzly bear, the whooping crane, the trumpeter swan, all fall into this category. Some, like the mountain goat and the barren ground caribou, though a bit more adaptable, live in more remote habitats by choice, so suffer less battering by civilization. Still others, such as white-tailed deer and pronghorn antelope, have shown unexpected adaptability and now thrive even where man is a daily presence.

Despite the lessons learned and the constructive steps taken over the past 75 years, this has not been a good century for many wildlife species in America, primarily because man has so tremendously

altered the environment. In addition to pesticides, structural changes have accelerated in the past 25 or 30 years. Channelization, urban expansion, road construction, and land development, with their draglines and bulldozers have made inroads into wildlife habitat at an unprecedented rate.

Probably the single most destructive program is channelization—the elaborate effort of total water management schemes which has changed the face of most of the nation's major river systems. For decades now, dams and levees have been installed to control floods and assist navigation; potholes have been drained and river-valley timber has been removed to increase farm acreage and irrigation; streams have been straightened to make way for economic development of floodplains.

The massive sacrifice of wetlands habitat involved in the flood-control projects alone might have been acceptable if it had indeed insured the safety of human life and property. Unfortunately, it has not. A recent U.S. Government Accounting Office review of the problem stated that despite federal investment of some $9,000,000,000 since 1936, annual losses from floods are actually increasing.

The greatest wildlife habitat loss due to channelization has occurred along the vast Mississippi watershed and in the Southeast. The Kissimmee River which empties into Florida's Lake Okeechobee is an example of what can happen when a formerly meandering river is made into a straight ditch. The goal was to drain adjacent wetland for agriculture and for real estate development. The Kissimmee, no longer allowed to weave its way between grassy banks, now rushes its load of silt, fertilizer, and pesticides into the lake. To halt the inevitable deterioration of Okeechobee, which has reached serious proportions, the State of Florida is studying the possibility of making the Kissimmee back into a meandering river. That should slow the water flow, but it can never restore the centuries-old marshes which

Interest in wildlife grew in the 1940s, even taking comic-strip form. Cartoonist Ed Dodd's Mark Trail *has been popular since 1945. Recently he spotlighted the porpoise (opposite above), making the public more aware of species like the common dolphin (opposite below), now threatened by commercial tuna fishermen whose nets inadvertently snare and destroy these intelligent mammals.*

were once an integral part of the shore, and home to countless birds, fish, and amphibians.

Nor can one neglect mention of the strip miners' depredations. Having learned little from what happened in the Appalachians, we now face the possibility of strip mining of coal in the northern Great Plains. Beneath the relatively thin layer of topsoil in this grassland home of deer, pronghorn, sage hen, sharp-tailed grouse, and other game species, lie veins of coal that can readily be mined with the mammoth new machines created for strip mining.

Attempts have been made to reclaim both private and government lands elsewhere after they were strip mined. The replanting done thus far has taken little account of the diversity of plant life needed by both wildlife and domestic livestock. It is highly debatable whether reclamation can or will be successful on those western plains. With their scant annual rainfall—only 12 to 16 inches—an entirely new reclamation technology is called for. Large-scale strip mining could pollute or destroy natural springs, lower the water table, and alter the whole range of vegetation.

Man has changed wildlife habitat not only by his farming, lumbering, stream-altering, and mining methods, but also by monoculture. This planting of vast land areas to one crop—wheat, say, or corn, or cotton—does away with small fields and fence-rows. It rids the land of all those brushy corners with their variety of plants that have, since the first farmer tended a patch of grain, meant food and havens for wildlife. Perhaps that is one reason New England, populous as it is and urbanized so persistently, still has so much wildlife. For the most part hilly and rocky, it could not ever be plowed to the last acre. Crops are grown in patches, not in horizon-wide fields, and there are many margins that are perfect hideaways for wildlife.

A century ago the conservation effort was directed toward saving and encouraging game species, at first big game, and then the smaller game and wildfowl, particularly ducks and geese. The laws passed then and the refuges established undoubtedly saved many hunted species and gave them all a far better chance of survival. As the conservation movement progressed and as data were accumulated, wildlife management came to be recognized as essential to achieving and maintaining a healthy and healthful environment. Hunters and fishermen were, it became obvious, an essential part of the living-with-wildlife process. Those who took fish and game helped maintain a balance thrown completely askew by elimination of natural predators. Moreover, outdoor people saw that they had a stake in maintaining this environment too.

It also was evident, when the management programs had been carried out for a few years, that they were benefitting nongame species, and that they too were an essential part of the big picture. Bird-watching has become a national avocation; and that in itself is an index to our desire to regain contact with the wild. Nobody knows how many bird-watchers there are today, but they run well into the millions. Hunters and fishermen have increased from 32,000,000 in 1954 to 43,000,000 in 1974. Wildlife books, magazines, television programs—even comic strips detailing the ways of the wild—enjoy unprecedented popularity. Oil spills and other events affecting wildlife get a big play in the newspapers.

We have, in brief, become wildlife-conscious at the same time that we have become an urban people. More than 70 percent of Americans now live in cities. But there is a kind of race memory that inspires hope and belief that the country and its wildlife are still out there and will be forever.

We know that our cities are being smothered with fumes from automobiles, factories, and furnaces. We know that too many of our lakes are open cesspools and that our rivers are putrid with sewage, industrial effluents, and pesticides. We know that all these wastes are fouling our oceans, along with oil spills. But we want also to know that out there in the 80-odd percent of this land not yet urbanized there are clean air, clean water, open skies, and wildlife—birds that sing and soar and hatch healthy broods, fish that have fresh, clean water in which to spawn, deer and foxes and pronghorns that live a life of normal, natural hazards but still live. And we want to see them for ourselves whenever we can.

We want to save such places, and we want to save the wildlife that lives there. Not as a sampling, a reminder of the past, but as a part of a healthy, well-balanced environment of today.

We have learned to care.

"Out of Limbo" (trumpeter swan) by Walter A. Weber, 1942.

TRIUMPHS OF CONCERN

From the mists of extinction, the Labrador duck, passenger pigeon, Carolina parakeet, and flightless great auk watch the saved trumpeter swan wing toward its Red Rock Lakes Refuge in Montana. By such rescue operations, concerned Americans are bringing animals of field, forest, and stream into new centuries of life on this altered continent.

HEARING THE CRY OF THE PLUMED BIRDS

Arrayed in splendor that nearly spelled their doom, the reddish egret, roseate spoonbill, and snowy egret (like the magnificent trumpeter swan) fell to fashion's demand for feathers in the late 1800s. Milady powdered her nose with swansdown puff, fanned her brow with elegant pink spoonbill plumes, and blushed beneath a hatful of snow-white egret feathers—once nuptial plumes raised in filmy fans from the head, throat, and shoulders of courting birds. Ultimately laws protected the plumed birds, as fashion bowed to public outcry and private concern. On his own refuge in Louisiana, E. A. McIlhenny saved the snowy egret in 1892; "Ding" Darling, founder of the National Wildlife Federation, fought hard for the trumpeters' refuge and won a preservation cliffhanger; when Red Rock Lakes Refuge was created in 1935, it mustered only 46 swans; today they are found in scattered locations from the Pacific to Minnesota. This gallery by Walter A. Weber, Roger Tory Peterson, and Francis L. Jaques adorned National Wildlife Federation conservation stamps, reminding us all to guard wetland refuges where these elegant birds now thrive.

Roseate spoonbill by Roger Tory Peterson, 1960; right, snowy egret by Francis Lee Jaques, 1944. Opposite: reddish egret by Walter A. Weber, 1948.

RESTORING GAME TO FOREST AND FIELD

"Make it our national bird," said Ben Franklin. The wild turkey was strong, smart, scrappy, and as captured here by Louis Agassiz Fuertes, handsome. This native bird was driven from much of its forest home by settlers' guns and axes. In the 1950s biologists transplanted remnant flocks to old restored habitats and to new woodlands where they flourish as of old. On the prairies, other game birds fled before the plow, never to return. Their niche was taken by China's ring-necked pheasant, introduced in Oregon in the 1880s. Today the pheasant, portrayed here by Ned Smith, abounds from coast to coast.

Wild turkey by Louis Agassiz Fuertes, 1910. Opposite: "Cock of the Fencerow" (ring-necked pheasant) by Ned Smith, 1973.

Reece

MULTIPLYING NATURE'S UNDERWATER BOUNTY

All they wanted, the Pilgrims told King James, was "leave to worship God ... and to catch fish." In America they gave thanks for noble trout leaping after minnows and insects in clear, cold streams. Generations of anglers matched wits with favorites, painted above by Ned Smith: from top to bottom, the cutthroat found by Lewis and Clark; the brook trout that fed Eastern pioneers; the West Coast's adaptable rainbow; and Europe's hardy brown, now at home in American rivers made muddy or warm by man's activities on the land. The canal that let parasitic sea lampreys into the Great Lakes imperiled lake trout like those opposite, painted by Maynard Reece, but today chemicals control the lamprey. And in hatcheries everywhere man lends nature a hand, raising trout from eggs to fingerlings and even larger, for the varied lakes and streams of America.

Top to bottom, cutthroat, brook, rainbow, and brown trout by Ned Smith, 1968-9. Opposite: lake trout by Maynard Reece, 1962.

ACCOMMODATING THE DEER FAMILY IN AN INDUSTRIALIZED LAND

It seemed a continent of antlered animals. Explorers found moose browsing in bogs, caribou feeding in northern wood and tundra, and everywhere white-tailed deer and wapiti, misnamed elk after Europe's look-alike. Western settlers found black-tailed and mule deer in the uplands, like the pair above vaulting through the ideal browse of an old burn in John Clymer's "Ridge Run." Like the forest fire, the white man gave new habitat to these forest-edge browsers as he carved fields from unbroken woodland. But he sorely needed meat and hides; settler and market hunter cut deeply into the herds until conservationists brought law and science to the rescue. As for the magnificently racked elk opposite, artist Guy Coheleach met him face-to-face in the Rockies, last stronghold of once-depleted herds. Overprotected at first in park and preserve until its migrations were understood and its grazing rights respected, the elk enjoys new security. As wildlife managers seek neither to overprotect nor overhunt, elk prosper in western foothills and mountain meadows—and deer roam more widely than ever.

"Ridge Run" (black-tailed deer) by John Clymer, 1965. Opposite: wapiti stag by Guy Coheleach, 1972.

LEARNING TO RESPECT THEIR MAJESTIES' REALMS

*The spectacle of a moose swinging a six-foot rack, the
frozen poise of watchful bighorn sheep, the crosscurrents of
fear and fascination as hiker spots grizzly—these are moments
few ever know, captured by artists Clark Bronson, Douglas
Allen, and Maynard Reece. Even when America was young,
these animals of deep forests and mountain peaks were largely
unknown, except by explorers scouting new terrain or loggers
cutting into virgin stands. The moose, once driven northward,
we now coax back by sound forest husbandry. Herders drove
domestic sheep into bighorn country and market hunters
took heavy toll. Today the bighorn is being reintroduced
to its former haunts. And what of the territorial instincts
we rile, camping in a grizzly's domain? By tagging and radio
tracking, zones of mutual safety are established. But the
needs of some big game animals have always been absolute:
wilderness so vast that they can find food and cover, choose
mates, and bear young which may never see a human.*

Grizzly bear by Maynard Reece, 1965; above, "Among the Clouds" (bighorn sheep)
by Douglas Allen, 1966. Opposite: "Startled Bull Moose" by Clark Bronson, 1961.

KEEPING OUR COVENANT
WITH THE WILDLIFE WORLD

Admiral of a frolicking fleet, the sea otter painted by Ed Bierly steers a steady course back from the rim of extinction. Laws and treaties guard it from hunters; along California's coast and in a 2,700,000-acre refuge in Alaska its numbers increase.

"Sea Otters in the Aleutians" by Ed Bierly, 1973.

Much of America's wildlife beauty is intact and is being sustained—in refuges and parks, in hatcheries, in cleaner waters and restored habitats. If we so will it, backing up research with vigilant law and care, we may yet record wildlife's finest hour.

An Enduring Place
for Wildlife

As if it were a folktale, we keep retelling the story of the Welsh miners who would take a canary in a small wire cage down into the depths of the earth with them. As long as the bird hopped about within the cage, they were safe; if it faltered and died, the air was bad and they should clear out. We keep retelling the story because of its basic truth, that we rely on animals as indicators of the world's health. A recent example of this was the use of the chimp Ham in 1961 as a pre-astronaut to test the safety of space flight capsules. We Americans, animals all, are in this cosmic adventure of life together—a fact that we know in the back of our heads but have only gradually begun to recognize in the front of our minds.

In his centuries of life in America man has found the means to alter the environment to his own advantage in myriad ways. He has learned to cut trees and clear land, to plant and reap, to dig in the earth —even probe the ocean—for fuel and metals. He has discovered how to dredge ditches for drainage and to dam rivers for power. He has found ways to domesticate animals and plants, to breed new varieties more adaptable to his needs, and to increase crop yields. He has discovered the secret of gathering more fish from the waters and more flesh and fibers from animals and plants that share this environment with him. But even now, entering this final quarter of the twentieth century, man does not completely understand the natural forces around him and how they work together to form this environment. He has the power to alter it, even disastrously, but he doesn't have ultimate control over it. Man remains a part of nature, not the master of it.

An example of the unexpected turns environmental problems can take even when they are being carefully monitored is the mining waste disposal dilemma faced by the communities along the western shore of Lake Superior. As the rich iron ore of northern Minnesota was worked out 25 years or more ago, a new process was developed to recover black magnetic iron from low-content taconite. The rock is ground to a powder and mixed with water into a slurry from which the iron is removed by a magnetic field, but this leaves vast quantities of finely powdered rock and water to be disposed of. In 1947 the Reserve Mining Company proposed to build a plant at Silver Bay and to dump this slurry

Expanded offshore oil drilling is unpopular with most environmentalists. Oil slicks threaten estuarine wildlife like the grebe above, and onshore impact from associated heavy industry can be equally disastrous. Paradoxically, sport fishing has improved; underwater platform legs form artificial reefs which host marine life and attract fish (below). Specially adapted to grind barnacles are the teeth of the parrotfish (right.)

into Lake Superior, whose water hitherto had been clean enough to drink without treatment. Lake fishermen objected. Hunters and stream fishermen protested the company's alternate proposal—pumping the slurry inland into natural basins—because they feared it would affect trout streams and might even bury deer wintering-yards. By 1956 permits had been issued for the lake-dumping plan, and soon over 60,000 tons of colloidal rock flour were being discharged into Lake Superior every day.

By 1970 a delta of the rock discharge was visible in the 600-foot-deep water which had acquired a greenish tint, but repeated testing proved no damage beyond doubt to either the fish in the water or to the humans drinking it. Then in 1972 a member of the Save Lake Superior Association happened to ask a fateful question. Arlene Lehto, who had heard about asbestos pollution causing stomach cancer in Japan, wondered if this slurry might contain asbes-

tos-like fibers. Researchers found that it did, and that the fibers might be making the waters of the lake dangerous for people as well as for fish. The courts then gave the company one year (until March, 1976) to come up with a suitable land-disposal plan for veritable mountains of powdered rock.

Such unforeseen consequences of man's attempts to wrest a good life from the earth and its waters are being uncovered all too frequently. The past ten years have seen steadily mounting concern about cumulative, worldwide effects of growing populations, industrialization, testing of atomic devices, and use of pesticides. One reason is that the air forms a global envelope made up of powerful currents constantly in motion. When we set off an atomic blast over Nevada, the first evidence of fallout reached Europe in a matter of days. Another reason is that the oceans wash the shores of every continent. One of the most disturbing discoveries

in recent years was finding DDT in the wildlife of both the Arctic and Antarctic where the pesticide had not been used. So today international conferences are held about what's happening to the air we breathe and the oceans around us.

The first United Nations conference on these concerns was held in Stockholm in 1972. It was only a beginning, but it officially recognized environmental problems as global issues. The conference led participating nations to place restrictions on ocean dumping of toxic substances and on inter-

Long isolated, the polar bear now faces human invasion of its energy-rich domain. Little is known of these bears— total numbers are still only estimated—and such enigmas as their ability to traverse monotonous terrain through months of darkness remain unexplained. Polar-bear countries recently agreed to step up research and pool data in an effort to save these magnificent nomads of the North.

national trade in endangered species of wildlife. It called for a ten-year moratorium on all commercial whaling. It established an ongoing U.N. Environmental Program of activities such as Earthwatch, a communications network through which nations pool environmental information. Of the 113 governments represented at Stockholm, a majority has established at least the beginnings of national environmental policies and the governmental machinery to implement them.

Here at home, public response to warnings about wildlife problems and environmental dangers has quickened materially since Earth Day April 22, 1970. Some called that idealistic event the beginning of "the environmental revolution." It wasn't the beginning by any means, but it certainly was a turning point in conservation history. It launched new organizations and recharged old ones, brought forth new books and magazines, generated fresh leadership from the grassroots to the national level. The crusade shows few signs of abating. In a recent Gallup study about half of those interviewed said they would modify their way of living if it would improve environmental quality.

Congress responded to the public's new sense of urgency with a spate of environmental laws. Among the solid gains for wildlife achieved since Earth Day, especially in preserving and improving habitat, are the following legislative provisions:

- enlargement of the National Wilderness System, originally established by Congress in 1964, to a total of over 12,000,000 acres
- establishment of national parks, lakeshores, seashores, recreation areas, scenic rivers, refuges
- moratorium on the taking and importation of marine mammals except for federally supervised commercial harvest, research, and special uses
- payments for improving small woodlots
- payments for maintaining wetlands and retiring agricultural acres where waterfowl may feed
- grants to states which engage in long-range planning for coastal lands
- new tax on bows and arrows, and existing tax on handguns added to Wildlife Restoration Fund
- continued federal funds to increase anadromous fish, including operation of state hatcheries

- increased penalties for shooting eagles
- a ban on shooting wildlife from aircraft
- a ban on dumping hazardous substances in coastal areas and initiation of permit system for dumping other wastes in ocean waters

In addition to all these Congressional actions, President Nixon in 1970 set up the Environmental Protection Agency to coordinate many old environmental programs and to administer new ones. In 1972 the president issued an executive order banning the use of poisons on public lands. In the last two years the Environmental Protection Agency banned aldrin and dieldrin, and hearings are underway on the suspension of chlordane and heptachlor.

But of all recent governmental actions relating to the environment, the National Environmental Policy Act of 1969 (NEPA) opened the door to the most sweeping changes for wildlife. The law set up in the Executive Office of the President a Council on Environmental Quality to which all federal agencies are required to submit an environmental impact statement before they act on any major project affecting the environment. Gradually, conservation organizations have discovered the powerful new role this impact provision gives them in the decision-making process. Instead of learning about a proposed new dam or highway when bulldozers start to clear the land, they may now study and publicly discuss the anticipated environmental impact of a proposed project before construction begins.

The discovery by housewives, doctors, wildlife experts, economists, and sportsmen of the power which Congress, through NEPA, has handed to them has in turn had a tremendous impact on federal agencies. Some of the showdowns have ended up in court, making the environmental lawyer an important new member of the conservation team, with scientists and laymen playing supporting roles.

Even with primitive weapons, early whalers (opposite) took many sperm whales for blubber, oil, and ivory. Today, cannon harpoon guns (lower right) are equipped with delayed-action explosives, and air pump devices keep some shipside carcasses afloat. The South African vessel at lower left returns to port with a full cargo, despite pleas of conservation organizations for a moratorium on killing with which the United States has complied since 1972.

We are now at the point where conservation has a fresh opportunity to clarify its goals and count its forces. Very simply, the goal must be to find ways to save enough of the environment to make life livable for all of us. And that is where wildlife enters the picture so insistently. For wildlife is more than the sight of a deer at the edge of a farmer's woodlot or the sheer beauty of a golden eagle in flight; more than something to please bird-watchers and reward hunters. It is also one of the best indicators we have of the health of the environment.

In the front line of our attack force is the layman who is quick to recognize the significance of events going on around him. Such a man is Nathan Muskin of New Rochelle, New York. In 1972 he learned from former business associates that the U. S. Army had invited bids on 250,000 parkas, specifying that the ruffs be made of wolf fur. Alarmed at the prospect of such wholesale slaughter of what he knew to be an endangered animal in most of the lower 48 states, Mr. Muskin called the National Wildlife Federation in Washington. Explaining that he was blind, Mr. Muskin asked the Federation to intervene. It took only one letter to the Secretary of Defense to get the order for the wolf-fur trim switched to a synthetic fur then being developed. Mr. Muskin's telephone call is estimated to have saved the lives of 25,000 wolves, at least half of the wolf population of North America. Because the synthetic fur cost less, he also saved taxpayers over $1,000,000.

There are hundreds, perhaps thousands, of such individuals who seriously follow the conservation ideal without fanfare or financial reward. Among them are people like Dr. Robert Gammell and his wife Ann who band birds at the Des Lacs National Wildlife Refuge near their home in Kenmare, North Dakota. Dr. Gammell is a retired physician. Since 1957 the Gammells have banded over 190,000 birds

Early Spanish explorers in the Southwest did not depict "useless" arid regions on maps. Today, however, scientists appreciate deserts for the delicate and diverse life systems they support. The western diamondback rattler (top) is able to withstand temperature extremes of desert days and nights and obtain moisture from infrequent feedings. Jaws that unhinge can accommodate such sizeable prey as the jackrabbit (right), a desert speedster.

representing 224 species. This work, done on their own time and at their own expense, has played a part in the Denver Wildlife Research Center's study of blackbird numbers and migration patterns.

Then there are all the conservationist-consumers who heeded the 1973 call of America's leading conservation organizations to boycott Japanese and Russian goods until those two nations agreed to abide by International Whaling Commission quotas. The boycott was a last-ditch effort to wring compliance from the two major holdouts against the ten-year moratorium on whaling voted at the 1972 U. N. conference as well as against specific regulatory measures agreed to by IWC members.

Japanese and Russian whaling fleets take about 80 percent of the world's annual catch of approximately 40,000 whales, chiefly in North Pacific and Antarctic waters. At the 1975 meeting of the International Whaling Commission Japan and Russia finally agreed with other members not only to reduce (by 20 percent) annual whale harvests, but to put all whales in all oceans under a program of scientific management. Thus one objective of the boycott has been reached, but some conservation organizations may continue the ban until the ten-year moratorium is also achieved.

As more citizens become involved in these conservation battles, they become increasingly appreciative of the crucial role of their strategists, the professional wildlife scientists. Each year the stakes grow higher in the judgments they are required to make on behalf of wildlife (and therefore of people). In Alaska, for example, back in 1970 when the vast pipeline project was first proposed, state and federal wildlife managers were faced with the responsibility of evaluating a request for a right-of-way permit to lay a pipeline across 798 miles of wilderness from Prudhoe Bay to the port of Valdez. The 48-inch pipe would carry up to 2,000,000 barrels of

Radio tracking has advanced wildlife management a giant step. Signals sent by tiny devices attached to animals like the wolf opposite are received through antennae (lower right), providing vital data on species otherwise difficult to observe. Thus transplanted animals can be "watched." Aided by the helicopter, another modern management tool, biologists drive a herd of Yellowstone elk (top) into pens for removal to depleted ranges.

oil each day, and the oil would be at a temperature of 180 degrees Fahrenheit.

While recognizing the need for oil, the wildlife managers could also foresee the possible destruction of tundra, the blockage of caribou migration routes, the siltation of streams from road cuts, the interruption of runs of salmon, potential damage to duck nesting areas, and always the possibility of pipeline breaks. With the pipeline route crossing mountain ranges and river valleys, even the big game animals could be affected. Finally, the wildlife men knew that long after the oil exploitation ended, the natives would need the land, water, and wildlife resources for their livelihood.

So, concerned by inadequacies in the first environmental impact evaluations and in the engineering plans for withstanding earthquakes, protecting permafrost, and strengthening pipe-joint welds, an expanded team of wildlife managers and other specialists took four full years to study the plans and help determine the route and the construction methods which would have the least adverse impact on wildlife. The managers now inspect and monitor construction to see that stipulations are followed.

The comprehensiveness of the Alaskan assignment is a far cry from the work of the first wildlife managers back in the 1930s. Most of them were university professors of botany, biology, or zoology, expected chiefly to know the natural history and to improve the habitat of the animals under their care, and to schedule hunting and fishing seasons. Today we have around 20,000 wildlife and fisheries managers employed by state and federal agencies, private companies, and organizations. They still must know the life cycles of their wild charges and how to take censuses in the field, appraise quantity and quality of food resources, help to control problem species, tabulate kills by predators and hunters, and consult with specialists about the effects of pesticides. Many do some law enforcement work and carry on a broad program of public education.

With regrettable frequency the responsibilities of some wildlife experts include the ultimate task of finding ways to bring endangered species back from the brink of extinction. Among techniques now being used are captive breeding and restocking in the wild, setting aside of special wildlife habitat areas, and live trapping and transplanting.

The energy crisis has dimmed somewhat the high hopes raised on the first national Earth Day. In the long view it has also made us realize how completely everything has changed since the early settlement of our nation. The unlimited has turned out to be limited after all. Here we are in a finite world with only so much living space. Wherever food has been ample and modern medicine has flourished, the human population has turned out to be almost as explosive as are animal populations when the natural predators are eliminated. Famine occurs despite the Green Revolution that has increased food production in some parts of the world. Now it is evident that there will be famine whenever man overpopulates his environment. We in America have been fortunate thus far.

Our program must continue to be one of management and wise use, keeping as much as we can handle well, and preventing total destruction of any species—bird, beast, fish, flower, bush, or tree.

For some species, management means providing wilderness, the privacy and the natural growth, cover as well as food, that only a wilderness can provide. The California condor is a classic example. This rare bird of which only 40 or 50 survive must not be disturbed by man. The noise of his machines will cause the condors to desert nest, egg, chick, the area itself, and they lay only one egg a year. So we must make the choice—save wilderness areas or sacrifice wilderness species of wildlife.

For those species that can live close to man and his works, man must make certain allowances; otherwise conditions become intolerable for wildlife. Most lumber company lands, for example, like the farmer's woodlot and lower pasture, are havens for more wild animals than the uninitiated would suspect.

The small bog down the road from my farm was, until an outlander began filling it "because it attracts mosquitoes," a nursery and home for ducks, herons, muskrats, half a dozen species of frogs including spring peepers, and nobody knows how many insects, including several particularly beautiful dragonflies. All such wetlands, small and large, fresh and salt, must be saved for the welfare of their wildlife inhabitants, and for our own health.

All of our brooks, our rivers, our lakes too must eventually be cleaned up, or we admit defeat and live the rest of our polluted lives tolerating filthy water, perhaps even smelling the stench in our dooryards, no matter where we live. The same is true of our air, which not only filters the sunlight and heat but sustains our blood, our lungs, our heart, all our vital functions. And those of every breathing thing on earth, remember, from trees to tadpoles, from ants and bees to porpoises and whales.

With everyone aware of these things, at least dimly, we must check our impulses and refrain from exploiting the environment solely for financial profits. Few countries in the world still have as much as we have. We cannot afford to pauperize ourselves in terms of natural habitat as parts of Europe and much of Asia have done. That way lies irreparable damage. We now know this whole planet is a place of vast resources but not of limitless resources. We know it can support billions of people but not constantly increasing billions. We know it naturally is a beautiful and healthful habitat for us and for all forms of life, but that it can be poisoned, devastated, even depopulated, by man's arrogance, his stupidity, or his carelessness.

Man came here with the prehistoric animals from Asia across a land bridge created by a whim of the earth's climate. He came here from Europe, long, long afterward, looking for a fish, a beaver pelt, and a pot of gold. He found everything that he was looking for and more, much more. He once was one with the bear and the wolf, with the codfish and the whale. Now he must remember his beginnings here, and the trees, the vastness of woodlands, and the rivers of fresh water roaring to the sea, and the mountains that lifted his spirits and challenged his courage and bred the clouds that watered the valleys he would plow and plant. He must remember the plains dark with buffalo, the skies filled with pigeons, the beaver and mink and otter in the streams, the startling beauty and amazing speed and grace of the pronghorns, the yipping of prairie dogs, the night singing of the coyotes. He must remember deer and elk without number, and panthers, and grizzlies, and the echoing, gabbling call of wild turkey gobblers.

Remembering, he must be thankful that he still knows them all, and must resolve to pass on what he inherited from this land. Otherwise man too, though he survives another thousand years, will become a vanishing species.

Fishing for rainbow trout, Eagle Creek Punchbowl, Oregon.

WILDLIFE
IN OUR LIVES

*Yesterday he installed mufflers or sold insurance or ran a corporation. Tomorrow
he'll teach Sunday school or prune the hedge. Today he's in Oregon's Eagle
Creek Punchbowl—gone fishin', alone with his thoughts and nature's world.
In that wildlife world many pursue knowledge and some even find their life's work.*

A NICHE FOR EVERY NOVICE

*They've been quiet, patient, motionless—qualities not always found in young boys.
At 12,000 feet on New Mexico's Pecos Baldy they claim their hard-earned reward, a
staring match with two shy bighorn sheep. Incredibly, the sheep linger almost an hour,
leaving cloven hoofprints stamped indelibly in two growing minds. Would the lads trade
places with bird-watchers aboard the Whooping Crane in Texas? Perhaps so, for the
crane is surely a much rarer sight. Myriad moments like these await amateur naturalists
in the wild, whether in a group or on their own. Those boys below aren't scientists
at all—only dabblers. But they can tell you of wonders to be found in water dipped from
a Colorado mountain stream, or in the eye of a Clark's nutcracker as it snatches a proffered
peanut. In nature there's room for us all if we will seek it.*

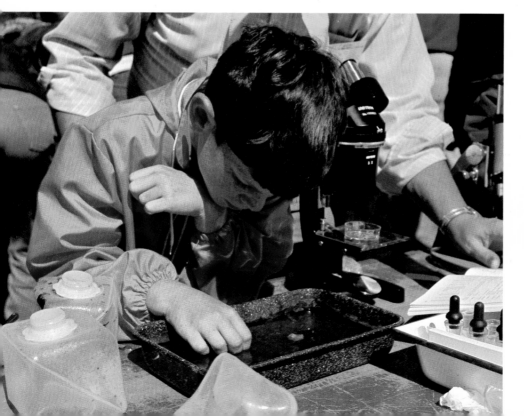

Desert bighorn sheep, Pecos Wilderness, New Mexico. Opposite: clockwise, whooping cranes, Aransas National Wildlife Refuge, Texas; Clark's nutcracker, Rocky Mountain National Park, Colorado; water pollution class, Conservation Summit, Estes Park, Colorado.

ZOOS: MORE THAN MEETS THE EYE

Ah-h-h-h! A cool snort on a hot day delights the elephant-watchers at the National Zoo in Washington, D.C. Mesopotamians at the far side of history kept zoos, islands of wildlife amid the bustle of their cities. Today's zoos, like today's cities, are a far cry from theirs—and some are a far cry from ours of a generation ago. Once we peered through stout bars to watch a lion pad endlessly to and fro. Now we often gaze at great cats prowling freely beyond a moat; with a little imagination we stand not in San Diego but on Serengeti. In yesterday's zoos endangered species found haven, but little else. Today Sabtu the orang-utan looks from keeper Bill Groth's arms to a brighter future; she was born and reared in zoos, living labs where scientists put their findings to work in breeding preserves apart from the crowds. No throngs ooh and ahh as zoologist James Mead of the Smithsonian Institution dissects a beached whale—but his studies help the living to survive. The crowd-pleasers are still the slow-motion elephant, the haughty lion, and the antic ape. Yet in some zoos we gaze longest at animals which can no longer survive in their natural habitat.

James Mead, Smithsonian Institution, measuring pilot whale; right, Bill Groth, Milwaukee County Zoo, holding orang-utan. Opposite: African elephant, National Zoo, Washington, D.C.

HOME IS THE HUNTER

When civilized man strode into the light of history, there was a falcon on his fist; he was a hunter then and had been for thousands of years. We humans have probably been predators for 99 percent of our tenure on the planet. Americans no longer need to kill for food, as did the pioneers; we no longer hunt for profit, as did the market hunters whose depredations helped erase whole species. But millions of us still hunt—and other millions wonder why. How, they ask, can you kill what you claim to love? And how can the hunters explain? They are the predators who keep herds in trim; the providers whose licenses and taxes pay for refuges and research. They have included such men as Ernest Hemingway, hunter and conservationist, and Morely Nelson, world renowned falconer who helped found a haven for raptors in Idaho's Snake River Canyon. For them and millions more, the thrill is not the kill but the hunt and the feast. And the hunt is a homecoming, a return to a wild world and a role that have shaped our species through time unimaginable.

Morely Nelson with prairie falcon, Snake River Birds of Prey Natural Area, Idaho; left, setting decoys, Currituck Sound, North Carolina. Opposite: Hemingway and family near Dietrich, Idaho.

DOWN TO THE SEA IN SCUBA GEAR

Beneath the ocean's gauzy ceiling we live and breathe only as our machines allow. Yet even in the sea we are in our ancient home, for here life began, diversified, and at last colonized the land. And the sea is at home in us, its blend of salts closely mirrored in our own bloodstream. The sea may yet nurture life in new ways as we probe its secrets and learn new ways to tap its limitless bounty. The biologist below has speared a barracuda for further study, perhaps to unravel the mystery of why its flesh sometimes turns toxic for those who regard it as a delicacy. No such subtle time bomb imperils the photographer opposite; if these silky sharks attack—as sharks seldom do—his peril will be immediate. As researchers learn its ways, the sea becomes safer for those who plunge purely for pleasure, like the diver at right surrounded by marine life in an underwater park.

Spearing barracuda, reef off Miami, Florida; above, examining yellow grunts and brain coral, John Penny Camp Coral Reef State Park, Florida. Opposite: photographing silky sharks, Tongue of the Ocean, Andros Island, Bahamas.

REWARDS WHERE TWO WORLDS MEET

The shore is a world of fun for families on a lazy afternoon—beachcombing, wading, watching birds of shore and sea. Here we can have our fun and eat it too, as the succulent clam spouts from a hole in the sand and the pugnacious crab scuttles sideways through the shallows. Storm and wave donate driftwood for a fire; sun and cloud scorch the evening sky with a fire all their own. A new tide will erase our footprints, just as tides long ago rubbed out the tracks of Americans foraging here in the endless search for food. Some still search— and make their living from the catch. From slatted traps they harvest the delectable lobster, checking first for size and weight, tossing back any that don't measure up. The rest of us search for understanding, for renewal, for the wisdom that will keep our planet safe for all its tenants. In our search we turn, and return, to the wild places of the earth, drawn by our kinship with the creatures who have shared our walk through time.

Clamming, Wellfleet Beach, Cape Cod, Massachusetts. Opposite: from top, measuring lobster catch, Mt. Desert Island, Maine; steaming crabs, Salmon Creek Beach, Bodega, California.

Surplus military land on Georgia's Harris Neck caught the eye of the National Wildlife Refuge System in 1962. The area's acres range from oak stands and bottomland to teeming salt marshes. The land hosts great numbers of deer, turkeys, fox squirrels, land and water birds, alligators—even bobcats and river otters. Now resident Canada geese patrol the ghostly airstrip as it awaits the seasonal touchdown of other migratory birds and the arrival of visitors who come to view this 2,700-acre refuge, one small parcel of America's vast wildlife lands.

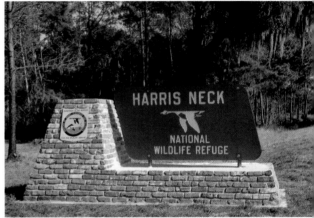

Appendix

For readers who want to broaden their knowledge of American wildlife by firsthand observation, the editors have prepared the following summary of wildlife habitat data including maps and sources of additional information on pages 194-198.

HOW MUCH WILDLIFE HABITAT DO WE HAVE?

While we have set aside approximately 34,000,000 acres as wildlife refuges where the largest flocks and herds may be observed, wildlife is all about us, sharing most of the 2,300,000,000 acres of land and water which make up our nation's fundamental resource base. These forests, farmlands, mountains, deserts, lakes, and rivers give us all of our food, water, shelter, and recreation. They are also the only available habitats for the 2,100-plus species of vertebrate animals which share this country with us.

WHO OWNS OUR WILDLIFE LANDS?

The federal government still controls approximately 761,000,000 acres, one-third of the total area of the United States. Since these are largely undeveloped lands located chiefly in the western states, they provide vast sweeps of habitat for animals of the West. The specific custodians of most of these lands are the following government agencies:

U.S. Department of the Interior:
Bureau of Land Management	451,000,000 acres
Fish and Wildlife Service	34,000,000 acres
National Park Service	29,000,000 acres
Bureau of Reclamation	8,000,000 acres

U.S. Department of Agriculture
Forest Service	187,000,000 acres

U.S. Department of Defense
Depts. of Army, Navy, Air Force	23,000,000 acres
U.S. Army Corps of Engineers	7,000,000 acres

The most familiar types of federal lands managed by these landlords are national parks, national forests, and national wildlife refuges. Less well known are the national resource lands of the Bureau of Land Management, the conservation acres developed by the military departments, and the wilderness areas which have been designated by Congress in accordance with the Wilderness Act of 1964. (Wilderness areas are created out of lands already in the national forests, national parks, and national wildlife refuges in order to give those specified areas more protection from the impact of man).

In the 200 years since our independence was won, nearly 2,500,000 acres of our land have been settled by homesteaders, and other millions of acres have been transferred by Congress to states, to railroads, and to private groups. Altogether, approximately 1,145,000,000 acres have passed into private hands. This is where most of our wildlife lives. In states east of the Missouri River rabbits, squirrels, raccoons, mourning doves, quail, opossums, and even deer thrive in cultivated fields, privately owned woodlots, and in residential backyards.

WHO CARES FOR OUR WILDLIFE?

Under the U.S. Constitution responsibility for all wildlife—fishes, amphibians, reptiles, birds, mammals—rests with the states. This includes those found on all the national refuges, parks, forests, and other federal lands, as well as on state and private property. One exception is responsibility for migratory birds which is vested in the U.S. Fish and Wildlife Service. There are also a few localities where state jurisdiction has been ceded to the federal government, and a few national parks like Yellowstone which were created before adjacent territories became states.

WHO PAYS FOR WILDLIFE CARE?

To cover the costs of wildlife research, buying refuges, building marshes and dams, creating boat-launching sites, and enforcing laws, the states expend funds received from the sale of hunting and fishing licenses, and from federal excise taxes on some types of fishing tackle, hunting arms and ammunition, and bows and arrows. In 1974, a record 43,475,000 sportsmen paid over $270,000,000 for these licenses plus an additional $75,000,000 in manufacturer's excise taxes. In addition, federal parks, forests, and refuges, in contrast to state areas, receive annual appropriations from Congress. Counties, townships, and municipalities also share the cost of looking after the wildlife on the watersheds and recreation areas they own.

NATIONAL WILDLIFE REFUGES

The purpose of our National Wildlife Refuge System is to provide sanctuary for nesting and migrating waterfowl and other migratory birds, fishes, some big game animals, and several endangered or threatened species. Their varied habitat needs are met on 355 migratory bird refuges; 16 big game areas; 4 national game ranges, and 4 national wildlife ranges. Most of the refuges are on federal lands controlled by the U.S. Fish and Wildlife Service.

In addition, there are more than 1,370,000 acres of wetlands known as waterfowl production areas. These are located primarily in the "pothole country" of Minnesota, the Dakotas, eastern Montana, and Nebraska, and they have been purchased with funds from the sale of duck stamps to hunters, conservationists, and stamp collectors.

Each year the 379 units in the refuge system attract more than 21,000,000 visitors. Nearly all refuges are open to bird-watchers and other wildlife-oriented activities, including fishing and controlled public hunting in some instances.

For information on federal fish and wildlife refuge programs, establishments, and landholdings, contact the Regional Director, U.S. Fish and Wildlife Service, at the following addresses:

Pacific Region (CA, HI, ID, NV, OR, WA): 1500 Plaza Bldg., 1500 N.E. Irving St., Portland, OR 97208

Southwest Region (AZ, NM, OK, TX): Federal Bldg., U.S. Post Office and Court House, 500 Gold Ave. S.W., Albuquerque, NM 87103

North Central Region (IL, IN, MI, MN, OH, WI): Federal Bldg., Fort Snelling, Twin Cities, MN 55111

Southeast Region (AL, AR, FL, GA, KY, LA, MS, NC, SC, TN): 17 Executive Park Dr., Atlanta, GA 30329

Northeast Region (CT, DE, ME, MD, MA, NH, NJ, NY, PA, RI, VT, VA, WV): John M. McCormack Post Office and Courthouse, Boston, MA 02109

Alaska Area (AK): 813 D St., Anchorage 99501

Denver Region (CO, IA, KS, MO, MT, NB, ND, SD, UT, WY): 10597 W. 6th Ave., Denver 80215

NATIONAL RESOURCE LANDS

Public domain lands which have never been transferred to private ownership nor withdrawn for parks, refuges, or other federal purposes, are now called national resource lands. Their big game populations help attract up to 90,000,000 recreation visits per year. Located mostly in the western states, herds are estimated at 1,500,000 deer, 180,000 antelope, 500,000 caribou, 158,000 elk, 35,000 bighorn sheep, 37,000 bear, and smaller numbers of moose, mountain goat, bison, and javelina.

Custodian of these 451,000,000 acres is the Bureau of Land Management which works closely with other state and federal agencies engaged in protection and enhancement of the habitat, and in providing access to hunting and fishing areas. Endangered species habitat receives priority attention.

The Bureau of Land Management is also responsible for mineral production, grazing, forest management, watershed protection, and industrial development on these lands. For additional information, permits for land use, and recreation opportunities, contact the State Director, Bureau of Land Management, at the following addresses:

AK: 555 Cordova St., Anchorage 99501

AZ: 2400 Valley Bank Center, Phoenix 85025

CA: Federal Office Bldg., Rm. E-2841, 2800 Cottage Way, Sacramento 95825

CO: Rm. 700, Colorado State Bank Bldg., 1600 Bdwy., Denver 80202

ID: 398 Federal Bldg., 550 W. Fort St., Boise 83724

MT: Federal Bldg., 316 N. 26th St., Billings 59101

NV: Federal Bldg., Rm. 3008, 300 Booth St., Reno 89502

NM: Federal Bldg., South Federal Place, Santa Fe 87501

OR and WA: 729 N.E. Oregon St., P.O. Box 2965, Portland, OR 97208

UT: Federal Bldg., 125 S. State, P.O. Box 11505, Salt Lake City 84111

WY: Jos. C. O'Mahoney Federal Center, Cheyenne 82001

Eastern States Office: 7981 Eastern Ave., Silver Spring, MD 20910

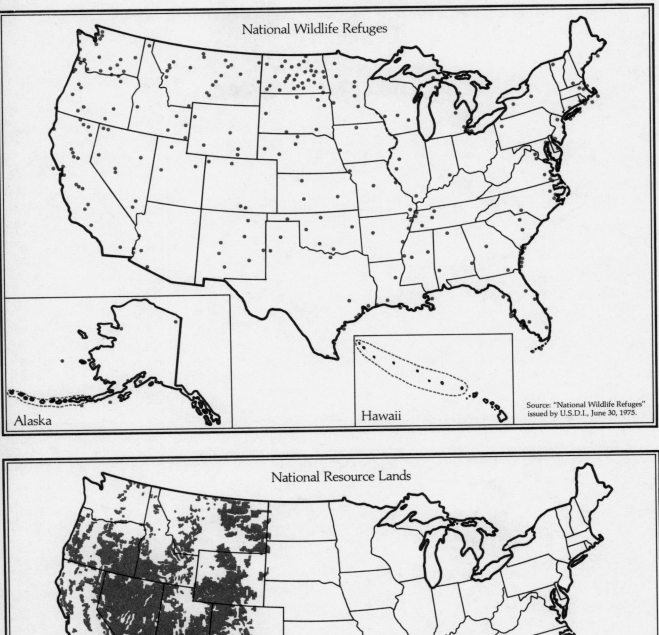

National Wildlife Refuges

Alaska

Hawaii

Source: "National Wildlife Refuges" issued by U.S.D.I., June 30, 1975.

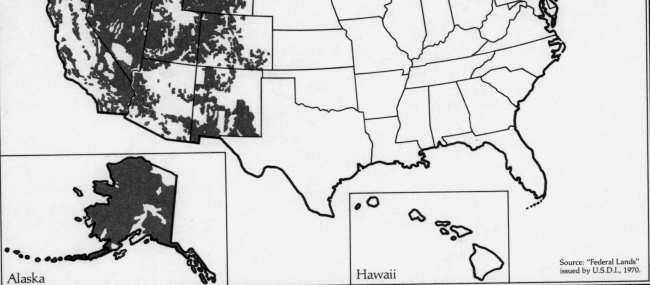

National Resource Lands

Alaska

Hawaii

Source: "Federal Lands" issued by U.S.D.I., 1970.

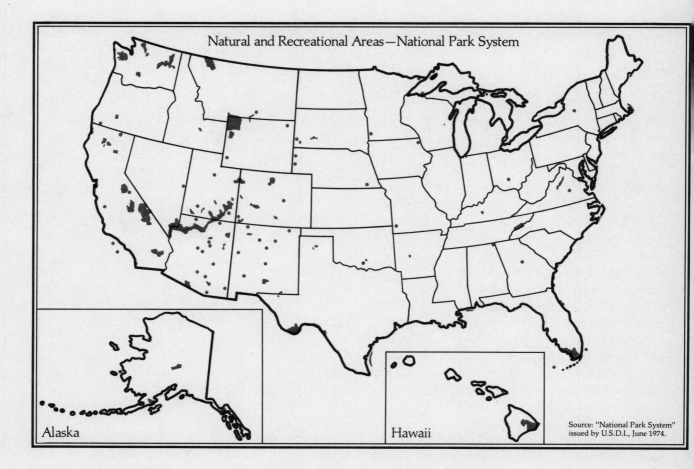

Natural and Recreational Areas—National Park System

Alaska

Hawaii

Source: "National Park System" issued by U.S.D.I., June 1974.

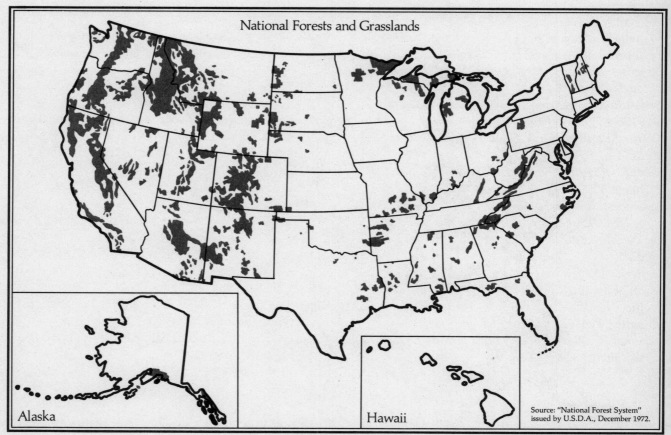

National Forests and Grasslands

Alaska

Hawaii

Source: "National Forest System" issued by U.S.D.A., December 1972.

NATIONAL PARK SYSTEM

With no little pride it can be reported that our national parks are ranked foremost among the leading park systems in the world. Its task: "to conserve the scenery and the natural and historic objects and the wildlife therein . . . by such means as will leave them unimpaired for the enjoyment of future generations." The National Park System presently consists of 74 natural areas, 45 recreational areas, and 166 historical areas in addition to the unique National Capital Parks in the Washington, D.C. metropolitan area. Visitations exceeded 217,000,000 in 1974. These outstanding places vary tremendously in natural features; in size they range from less than one acre for some of the historical sites to 2,800,000 acres for Glacier Bay National Monument in Alaska.

Tent and vehicle camp sites are abundant in the National Park System; other accommodations include guest rooms, cabins, and trailer hookups. Educational campfire talks, naturalist walks, and scientific displays are prominent features of the major park areas. Fishing is allowed, but little or no hunting. For specific information about the wildlife which may be seen in the parks, or about backpacking, winter and summer accommodations, and seasonal programs for visitors, inquire of the Regional Director, National Park Service, at the following regional offices:

Mid-Atlantic: 143 S. Third St., Philadelphia, PA 19106

North Atlantic: 150 Causeway St., Boston, MA 02114

Southeast: 1895 Phoenix Blvd., Atlanta, GA 30337

Midwest: 1709 Jackson St., Omaha, NB 68102

Southwest: Old Santa Fe Trail, P.O. Box 728, Santa Fe, NM 87501

Rocky Mountain: P.O. Box 25287, Denver, CO 80225

Western: 450 Golden Gate Ave., P.O. Box 36036, San Francisco, CA 94102

Pacific Northwest: Rm. 931, 1424 Fourth Ave., Seattle, WA 98101

National Capital Parks: 1100 Ohio Dr., S.W., Washington, DC 20242

NATIONAL FORESTS AND NATIONAL GRASSLANDS

The 155 national forests and 19 national grasslands located in 41 states and Puerto Rico are managed for a sustained yield of wood and forage; timber is processed into thousands of products and grasses feed 1,500,000 cattle and 1,700,000 sheep. Other uses are encouraged. Water from forested watersheds irrigates large agricultural areas. Habitat is provided for large and small mammals, birds, fishes, amphibians, and reptiles.

Recreation is available for hikers, campers, canoers, skiers, picnickers, hunters, and fishermen. Wildlife staff officers of the U.S. Forest Service cooperate with other federal and state wildlife officials in the enforcement of game laws and protection of wildlife resources. The wildlife officers also contribute to decisions on management of timber, rangelands, and other forest activities.

The visitor information service, interpretative facilities, campfire programs, and self-guiding tours emphasize data on the fish and wildlife of each forest area. For information on recreational opportunities and wildlife to be seen on specific forests and grasslands, contact the Regional Forester, U.S. Forest Service, at the following addresses:

Northern Region: Federal Bldg., Missoula, MT 59801

Rocky Mountain Region: 11177 W. 8th Ave., Box 25127, Lakewood, CO 80225

Southwestern Region: Federal Bldg., 517 Gold Ave. S.W., Albuquerque, NM 87102

Intermountain Region: Federal Bldg., 324 25th St., Ogden, UT 84401

California Region: 630 Sansome St., San Francisco, CA 94111

Pacific Northwest Region: 319 S.W. Pine St., P.O. Box 3623, Portland, OR 97208

Southern Region: 1720 Peachtree Rd., N.W., Atlanta, GA 30309 (Puerto Rico not shown on map)

Eastern Region: Clark Bldg., 633 W. Wisconsin Ave., Milwaukee, WI 53203

Alaska Region: Federal Office Bldg., Box 1628, Juneau, AK 99801

Fish and Game Commissions and Departments of the U.S. and Canada

All states and provinces have professional organizations for the study, protection, and management of fish and wildlife. They provide information upon request about fishing and hunting regulations, welfare of endangered species, habitat conditions, diseases of wild animals, and many other conservation-related topics.

Alabama Dept. of Conservation and Natural Resources, 64 N. Union St., Montgomery 36104

Alaska Dept. of Fish and Game, Subport Bldg., Juneau 99801

Arizona Game and Fish Dept., 2222 W. Greenway Rd., Phoenix 85023

Arkansas Game and Fish Commission, Game and Fish Commission Bldg., Little Rock 72201

California Dept. of Fish and Game, 1416 Ninth St., Sacramento 95814

Colorado Div. of Wildlife, 6060 Bdwy., Denver 80216

Connecticut Dept. of Environmental Protection, State Office Bldg., 165 Capitol Avenue, Hartford 06115

Delaware Dept. of Natural Resources and Environmental Control, Div. of Fish and Wildlife, The Edward Tatnall Bldg., Legislative Ave. & William Penn St., Dover 19901

District of Columbia Metropolitan Police, 300 Indiana Ave., NW, Washington 20001

Florida Game and Fresh Water Fish Commission, 620 S. Meridian, Tallahassee 32304

Georgia State Game and Fish Div., Trinity Washington Bldg., 270 Washington St., SW, Atlanta 30334

Guam Dept. of Agriculture, Div. of Fish and Wildlife, Agana 96910

Hawaii Dept. of Land and Natural Resources, Div. of Fish and Game, Box 621, Honolulu 96809

Idaho Fish and Game Dept., 600 S. Walnut, Box 25, Boise 83707

Illinois Dept. of Conservation, 602 State Office Bldg., Springfield 62706

Indiana Dept. of Natural Resources, Div. of Fish and Wildlife, 608 State Office Bldg., Indianapolis 46204

Iowa State Conservation Commission, State Office Bldg., 300 4th St., Des Moines 50319

Kansas Forestry, Fish and Game Commission, Box 1028, Pratt 67124

Kentucky Dept. of Fish and Wildlife Resources, Capitol Plaza Tower, Frankfort 40601

Louisiana Wildlife and Fisheries Commission, 400 Royal St., New Orleans 70130

Maine Dept. of Inland Fisheries and Game, State Office Bldg., 284 State St., Augusta 04330

Maryland Fish and Wildlife Administration, Natural Resources Bldg., Annapolis 21401

Massachusetts Div. of Fisheries and Game, 100 Cambridge St., Boston 02202

Michigan Dept. of Natural Resources, Mason Bldg., Lansing 48926

Minnesota Dept. of Natural Resources, Div. of Fish and Wildlife, 301 Centennial Bldg., 658 Cedar St., St. Paul 55155

Mississippi Game and Fish Commission, Robert E. Lee Office Bldg., 239 N. Lamar St., P.O. Box 451, Jackson 39205

Missouri Dept. of Conservation, P.O. Box 180, Jefferson City 65101

Montana Fish and Game Dept., Helena 59601

Nebraska Game and Parks Commission, P.O. Box 30370, 2200 N. 33rd, Lincoln 68503

Nevada Dept. of Fish and Game, Box 10678, Reno 89510

New Hampshire Fish and Game Dept., 34 Bridge St., Concord 03301

New Jersey Dept. of Environmental Protection, Div. of Fish, Game, and Shellfisheries, Labor and Industry Bldg., Box 1390, Trenton 88625

New Mexico Dept. of Game and Fish, State Capitol, Santa Fe 87503

New York Dept. of Environmental Conservation, Fish and Wildlife Div., 50 Wolf Rd., Albany 12201

North Carolina Wildlife Resources Commission, Albemarle Bldg., 325 N. Salisbury St., Raleigh 27611

North Dakota State Game and Fish Dept., 2121 Lovett Ave., Bismarck 58501

Ohio Dept. of Natural Resources, Div. of Wildlife, Fountain Square, Columbus 43224

Oklahoma Dept. of Wildlife Conservation, 1801 N. Lincoln, P.O. Box 53465, Oklahoma City 73105

Oregon State Wildlife Commission, Box 3503, Portland 97208

Pennsylvania Game Commission, P.O. Box 1567, Harrisburg 17120

Pennsylvania Fish Commission, P.O. Box 1673, Harrisburg 17120

Puerto Rico Dept. of Natural Resources, P.O. Box 5887, Puerta de Tierra Station, San Juan 00906

Rhode Island Dept. of Natural Resources, Div. of Fish and Wildlife, 83 Park St., Providence 02903

South Carolina Wildlife and Marine Resources Dept., Box 167, Columbia 29202

South Dakota Dept. of Game, Fish and Parks, State Office Bldg., Pierre 57501

Tennessee Wildlife Resources Agency, P.O. Box 40747, Ellington Agricultural Center, Nashville 37204

Texas Parks and Wildlife Dept., John H. Reagan Bldg., Austin 78701

Utah State Dept. of Natural Resources, Div. of Wildlife Resources, 1596 West N. Temple, Salt Lake City 84116

Vermont Agency of Environmental Conservation, Fish and Game Dept., Montpelier 05602

Virginia Commission of Game and Inland Fisheries, 4010 W. Broad St., Box 11104, Richmond 23230

Washington Dept. of Fisheries, 115 General Administration Bldg., and Washington Dept. of Game, 600 N. Capitol Way, Olympia 98504

West Virginia Dept. of Natural Resources, 1800 Washington St., East, Charleston 25305

Wisconsin Dept. of Natural Resources, Box 450, Madison 53701

Wyoming Game and Fish Dept., 5400 Bishop Blvd., Cheyenne 82001

CANADA

Alberta Dept. of Lands and Forests, Natural Resources Bldg., Edmonton T5K 2E1

British Columbia Dept. of Recreation and Conservation, Fish and Wildlife Branch, Parliament Bldgs., Victoria V8V 1X4

Manitoba Dept. of Mines, Resources, and Environmental Mgmt., Legislative Bldg., Winnipeg R3C OV8

New Brunswick Dept. of Natural Resources, Centennial Bldg., Fredericton

Newfoundland Dept. of Tourism, Wildlife Div., Confederation Bldg., St. Johns

Nova Scotia Dept. of Lands and Forests, Wildlife Div., Box 516, Kentville

Ontario Ministry of Natural Resources, Div. of Fish and Wildlife, Whitney Block, 99 Wellesley St., W. Toronto M7A 1W3

Prince Edward Island Environmental Control Commission, P.O. Box 2000, Charlottetown

Quebec Dept. of Tourism, Fish and Game, Place de la Capitale, 150 East, St. Cyrille Blvd., Quebec City G1R 4Y1

Saskatchewan Dept. of Tourism and Renewable Resources, Fisheries and Wildlife, Financial Bldg., Regina S4P 2H9

Yellowknife Dept. of Industry and Development, Govt. of the N.W.T., Yellowknife, N.W.T. XOE 1HO

Yukon Game Dept., Box 2703, Whitehorse, Yukon Territory

ENDANGERED AND THREATENED SPECIES LIST

Under federal law lists are kept of endangered species (those in danger of extinction) and of threatened species (those likely to become endangered), and conservation programs are provided for them. This state list includes only vertebrates, with whales added at the end. It is based on 1975 compilations of the Office of Endangered Species, U. S. Department of the Interior.

ALABAMA
Watercress Darter (Etheostoma nuchale) American Alligator (Alligator mississippiensis) Southern Bald Eagle (Haliaeetus l. leucocephalus) Bachman's Warbler (Vermivora bachmanii) Florida Panther (Felis concolor coryi) Red-cockaded Woodpecker (Dendrocopos borealis) Indiana Bat (Myotis sodalis)

ALASKA
Aleutian Canada Goose (Branta canadensis leucopareia) American Peregrine Falcon (Falco peregrinus anatum) Arctic Peregrine Falcon (Falco peregrinus tundrius)

ARIZONA
Arizona (Apache) Trout (Salmo apache) Humpback Chub (Gila cypha) Colorado River Squawfish (Ptychocheilus lucius) Mexican Duck (Anas diazi) Southern Bald Eagle (Haliaeetus l. leucocephalus) American Peregrine Falcon (Falco peregrinus anatum) Masked Bobwhite (Colinus virginianus ridgwayi) Yuma Clapper Rail (Rallus longirostris yumanensis) Sonoran Pronghorn (Antilocapra americana sonoriensis) Gila Topminnow (Poeciliopsis o. occidentalis)

ARKANSAS
Southern Bald Eagle (Haliaeetus l. leucocephalus) American Alligator (Alligator mississippiensis) Red-cockaded Woodpecker (Dendrocopos borealis) Indiana Bat (Myotis sodalis)

CALIFORNIA
Lahontan Cutthroat Trout (Salmo clarki henshawi) Paiute Cutthroat Trout (Salmo clarki seleniris) Tecopa Pupfish (Cyprinodon nevadensis calidae) Mohave Chub (Gila mohavensis) Owens Pupfish (Cyprinodon radiosus) Unarmored Threespine Stickleback (Gasterosteus aculeatus williamsoni) Desert Slender Salamander (Batrachoseps aridus) Blunt-nosed Leopard Lizard (Crotaphytus silus) Santa Cruz Long-toed Salamander (Ambystoma macrodactylum croceum) San Francisco Garter Snake (Thamnophis sirtalis tetrataenia) Santa Barbara Song Sparrow (Melospiza melodia graminea) California Brown Pelican (Pelecanus occidentalis californicus) Aleutian Canada Goose (Branta canadensis leucopareia) California Condor (Gymnogyps californianus) Southern Bald Eagle (Haliaeetus l. leucocephalus) American Peregrine Falcon (Falco peregrinus anatum) Yuma Clapper Rail (Rallus longirostris yumanensis) California Clapper Rail (Rallus longirostris obsoletus) Light-footed Clapper Rail (Rallus longirostris levipes) California Least Tern (Sterna albifrons browni) Morro Bay Kangaroo Rat (Dipodomys heermanni morroensis) Salt Marsh Harvest Mouse (Reithrodontomys raviventris) San Joaquin Kit Fox (Vulpes macrotis mutica)

COLORADO
Greenback Cutthroat Trout (Salmo clarki stomias) Colorado River Squawfish (Ptychocheilus lucius) American Peregrine Falcon (Falco peregrinus anatum) Black-footed Ferret (Mustela nigripes)

CONNECTICUT
Indiana Bat (Myotis sodalis)

DELAWARE
Southern Bald Eagle (Haliaeetus l. leucocephalus)

FLORIDA
Shortnose Sturgeon (Acipenser brevirostrum) Eastern Brown Pelican (Pelecanus occidentalis carolinensis) Florida Everglade Kite (Rostrhamus sociabilis plumbeus) Southern Bald Eagle (Haliaeetus l. leucocephalus) Dusky Seaside Sparrow (Ammospiza maritima nigrescens) Cape Sable Sparrow (Ammospiza maritima mirabilis) Florida Panther (Felis concolor coryi) Florida Manatee (Trichechus manatus latirostris) Key Deer (Odocoileus virginianus clavium) American Alligator (Alligator mississippiensis) Red-cockaded Woodpecker (Dendrocopos borealis) Okaloosa Darter (Etheostoma okaloosae) Indiana Bat (Myotis sodalis)

GEORGIA
American Alligator (Alligator mississippiensis) Eastern Brown Pelican (Pelecanus occidentalis carolinensis) Southern Bald Eagle (Haliaeetus l. leucocephalus) Florida Panther (Felis concolor coryi) Red-cockaded Woodpecker (Dendrocopos borealis) Indiana Bat (Myotis sodalis)

HAWAII
Hawaiian Dark-rumped Petrel (Uau) (Pterodroma phaeopygia sandwichensis) Hawaiian Goose (Nene) (Branta sandvicensis) Laysan Duck (Anas laysanensis) Hawaiian Duck (Koloa) (Anas wyvilliana) Hawaiian Hawk (Io) (Buteo solitarius) Hawaiian Gallinule (Alae ula) (Gallinula chloropus sandvicensis) Hawaiian Coot (Alae keokeo) (Fulica americana alai) Hawaiian Stilt (Aeo) (Himantopus himantopus knudseni) Hawaiian Crow (Alala) (Corvus tropicus) Small Kauai Thrush (Puaiohi) (Phaeornis palmeri) Large Kauai Thrush (Kauai omao) (Phaeornis obscurus myadestina) Molokai Thrush (Olomau) (Phaeornis obscurus rutha) Nihoa Millerbird (Acrocephalus kingi) Kauai Oo (Oo aa) (Moho braccatus) Crested Honeycreeper (Akohekohe) (Palmeria dolei) Akiapolaau (Hemignathus wilsoni) Kauai Akialoa (Hemignathus procerus) Kauai Nukupuu (Hemignathus lucidus hanapepe) Maui Nukupuu (Hemignathus lucidus affinis) Hawaii Akepa (Akepa) (Loxops c. coccinea) Maui Akepa (Akepuie) (Loxops coccinea ochracea) Oahu Creeper (Alauwahio) (Loxops m. maculata) Molokai Creeper (Kakawahie) (Loxops maculata flammea) Maui Parrotbill (Pseudonestor xanthophrys) Ou (Psittirostra psittacea) Laysan Finch (Psittirostra c. cantans) Nihoa Finch (Psittirostra cantans ultima) Palila (Psittirostra bailleui) Hawaiian Hoary Bat (Lasiurus cinereus semotus)

IDAHO
American Peregrine Falcon (Falco peregrinus anatum) Northern Rocky Mountain Wolf (Canis lupus irremotus) Grizzly Bear (Ursus arctos horribilis)

ILLINOIS
Indiana Bat (Myotis sodalis) Longjaw Cisco (Coregonus alpenae) in Lake Mich.

INDIANA
Indiana Bat (Myotis sodalis) Longjaw Cisco (Coregonus alpenae) in Lake Michigan

IOWA
Indiana Bat (Myotis sodalis)

KANSAS
Southern Bald Eagle (Haliaeetus l. leucocephalus)

KENTUCKY
Indiana Bat (Myotis sodalis) Red-cockaded Woodpecker (Dendrocopos borealis)

LOUISIANA
American Alligator (Alligator mississippiensis) Southern Bald Eagle (Haliaeetus l. leucocephalus) American Ivory-billed Woodpecker (Campephilus p. principalis) Eastern Brown Pelican (Pelecanus occidentalis carolinensis) Red-cockaded Woodpecker (Dendrocopos borealis) Red Wolf (Canis rufus)

MAINE
Eastern Cougar (Felis concolor cougar) Possible

MARYLAND
Maryland Darter (Etheostoma sellare) Southern Bald Eagle (Haliaeetus l. leucocephalus) Delmarva Peninsula Fox Squirrel (Sciurus niger cinereus) Indiana Bat (Myotis sodalis) Eastern Cougar (Felis concolor cougar) Possible

MASSACHUSETTS
Indiana Bat (Myotis sodalis)

MICHIGAN
Kirtland's Warbler (*Dendroica kirtlandii*) Eastern Timber Wolf (*Canis lupus lycaon*) Longjaw Cisco (*Coregonus alpenae*) in Lakes Michigan, Huron; Blue Pike (*Stizostedion vitreum glaucum*) in Lake Erie

MINNESOTA
Eastern Timber Wolf (*Canis lupus lycaon*)

MISSISSIPPI
American Alligator (*Alligator mississippiensis*) Southern Bald Eagle (*Haliaeetus l. leucocephalus*) Red-cockaded Woodpecker (*Dendrocopos borealis*) Mississippi Sandhill Crane (*Grus canadensis pulla*) Indiana Bat (*Myotis sodalis*)

MISSOURI
Indiana Bat (*Myotis sodalis*) Red-cockaded Woodpecker (*Dendrocopos borealis*) Southern Bald Eagle (*Haliaeetus l. leucocephalus*)

MONTANA
American Peregrine Falcon (*Falco peregrinus anatum*) Black-footed Ferret (*Mustela nigripes*) Northern Rocky Mountain Wolf (*Canis lupus irremotus*) Grizzly Bear (*Ursus arctos horribilis*)

NEBRASKA
Black-footed Ferret (*Mustela nigripes*)

NEVADA
Lahontan Cutthroat Trout (*Salmo clarki henshawi*) Pahranagat Bonytail (*Gila robusta jordani*) Moapa Dace (*Moapa coriacea*) Cui-ui (*Chasmistes cujus*) Devil's Hole Pupfish (*Cyprinodon diabolis*) Warm Springs Pupfish (*Cyprinodon nevadensis pectoralis*) Pahrump Killifish (*Empetrichthys latos*) American Peregrine Falcon (*Falco peregrinus anatum*)

NEW HAMPSHIRE
Eastern Cougar (*Felis concolor cougar*) Possible; Indiana Bat (*Myotis sodalis*)

NEW JERSEY
Southern Bald Eagle (*Haliaeetus l. leucocephalus*) Eskimo Curlew (*Numenius borealis*)

NEW MEXICO
Gila Trout (*Salmo gilae*) Mexican Duck (*Anas diazi*) Southern Bald Eagle (*Haliaeetus l. leucocephalus*) American Peregrine Falcon (*Falco peregrinus anatum*)

NEW YORK
Shortnose Sturgeon (*Acipenser brevirostrum*) Longjaw Cisco (*Coregonus alpenae*) in Lake Erie; Blue Pike (*Stizostedion vitreum glaucum*) in Lake Erie, possibly Lake Ontario; Eastern Cougar (*Felis concolor cougar*) Indiana Bat (*Myotis sodalis*)

NORTH CAROLINA
American Alligator (*Alligator mississippiensis*) Eastern Brown Pelican (*Pelecanus occidentalis carolinensis*) Southern Bald Eagle (*Haliaeetus l. leucocephalus*) Red-cockaded Woodpecker (*Dendrocopos borealis*) Indiana Bat (*Myotis sodalis*) Eastern Cougar (*Felis concolor cougar*) Possible

NORTH DAKOTA
Black-footed Ferret (*Mustela nigripes*)

OHIO
Indiana Bat (*Myotis sodalis*) Longjaw Cisco (*Coregonus alpenae*) in Lake Erie; Blue Pike (*Stizostedion vitreum glaucum*) in Lake Erie

OKLAHOMA
American Alligator (*Alligator mississippiensis*) Red-cockaded Woodpecker (*Dendrocopos borealis*) Indiana Bat (*Myotis sodalis*) Southern Bald Eagle (*Haliaeetus l. leucocephalus*)

OREGON
California Brown Pelican (*Pelecanus occidentalis californicus*) Aleutian Canada Goose (*Branta canadensis leucopareia*) American Peregrine Falcon (*Falco peregrinus anatum*) Columbian White-tailed Deer (*Odocoileus virginianus leucurus*) Northern Rocky Mountain Wolf (*Canis lupus irremotus*)

PENNSYLVANIA
Indiana Bat (*Myotis sodalis*) Eastern Cougar (*Felis concolor cougar*) Possible; Longjaw Cisco (*Coregonus alpenae*) in Lake Erie; Blue Pike (*Stizostedion vitreum glaucum*) in Lake Erie

RHODE ISLAND
Indiana Bat (*Myotis sodalis*)

SOUTH CAROLINA
American Alligator (*Alligator mississippiensis*) Eastern Brown Pelican (*Pelecanus occidentalis carolinensis*) Southern Bald Eagle (*Haliaeetus l. leucocephalus*) Eskimo Curlew (*Numenius borealis*) American Ivory-billed Woodpecker (*Campephilus p. principalis*) Bachman's Warbler (*Vermivora bachmanii*) Red-cockaded Woodpecker (*Dendrocopos borealis*) Indiana Bat (*Myotis sodalis*) Eastern Cougar (*Felis concolor cougar*) Possible

SOUTH DAKOTA
Black-footed Ferret (*Mustela nigripes*)

TENNESSEE
Southern Bald Eagle (*Haliaeetus l. leucocephalus*) Red-cockaded Woodpecker (*Dendrocopos borealis*) Indiana Bat (*Myotis sodalis*)

TEXAS
Big Bend Gambusia (*Gambusia gaigei*) Comanche Springs Pupfish (*Cyprinodon elegans*) Clear Creek Gambusia (*Gambusia heterochir*) Pecos Gambusia (*Gambusia nobilis*) Fountain Darter (*Etheostoma fonticola*) American Alligator (*Alligator mississippiensis*) Texas Blind Salamander (*Typhlomolge rathbuni*) Houston Toad (*Bufo houstonensis*) Eastern Brown Pelican (*Pelecanus occidentalis carolinensis*) Mexican Duck (*Anas diazi*) Southern Bald Eagle (*Haliaeetus l. leucocephalus*) Attwater's Greater Prairie Chicken (*Tympanuchus cupido attwateri*) Whooping Crane (*Grus americana*) Eskimo Curlew (*Numenius borealis*) American Ivory-billed Woodpecker (*Campephilus p. principalis*) Red Wolf (*Canis rufus*) Black-footed Ferret (*Mustela nigripes*)

UTAH
Humpback Chub (*Gila cypha*) Woundfin (*Plagopterus argentissimus*) Colorado River Squawfish (*Ptychocheilus lucius*) American Peregrine Falcon (*Falco peregrinus anatum*) Utah Prairie Dog (*Cynomys parvidens*)

VERMONT
Indiana Bat (*Myotis sodalis*) Eastern Cougar (*Felis concolor cougar*) Possible

VIRGINIA
Southern Bald Eagle (*Haliaeetus l. leucocephalus*) Bachman's Warbler (*Vermivora bachmanii*) Red-cockaded Woodpecker (*Dendrocopos borealis*) Indiana Bat (*Myotis sodalis*) Eastern Cougar (*Felis concolor cougar*) Possible

WASHINGTON
Aleutian Canada Goose (*Branta canadensis leucopareia*) American Peregrine Falcon (*Falco peregrinus anatum*) Columbian White-tailed Deer (*Odocoileus virginianus leucurus*) Northern Rocky Mountain Wolf (*Canis lupus irremotus*)

WEST VIRGINIA
Indiana Bat (*Myotis sodalis*) Eastern Cougar (*Felis concolor cougar*) Possible

WISCONSIN
Eastern Timber Wolf (*Canis lupus lycaon*) Indiana Bat (*Myotis sodalis*) Longjaw Cisco (*Coregonus alpenae*) in Lake Michigan

WYOMING
Humpback Chub (*Gila cypha*) Kendall Warm Springs Dace (*Rhinichthys osculus thermalis*) American Peregrine Falcon (*Falco peregrinus anatum*) Black-footed Ferret (*Mustela nigripes*) Northern Rocky Mountain Wolf (*Canis lupus irremotus*) Grizzly Bear (*Ursus arctos horribilis*)

PUERTO RICO
Puerto Rican Boa (*Epicrates inornatus*) Puerto Rican Plain Pigeon (*Columba inornata wetmorei*) Puerto Rican Parrot (*Amazona vittata*) Puerto Rican Whippoor-will (*Caprimulgus noctitherus*)

VIRGIN ISLANDS
Puerto Rican Boa (*Epicrates inornatus*)

WHALES
Blue Whale (*Balaenoptera musculus*) Bowhead Whale (*Balaena mysticetus*) Finback Whale (*Balaenoptera physalus*) Gray Whale (*Eschrichtius gibbosus*) Humpback Whale (*Megaptera novaeangliae*) Right Whale (*Eubalaena* spp.—*All Species*) Sei Whale (*Balaenoptera borealis*) Sperm Whale (*Physeter catodon*)

Library of Congress Cataloging in Publication Data
Borland, Hal Glen, 1900-
    The history of wildlife in America.
    Bibliography: p.
    Includes index.
    1. Natural history—United States.
2. United States—History. 3. Wildlife conservation—United States—History.
4. Man—Influence on nature—United States—History. I. Title.
QH104.B65   591.9'73   75-15494
ISBN O-912186-20-8

PICTURE CREDITS

Page 1: Buffalo Hunt painted on elk-skin, Montana Crow, Museum of the American Indian, Heye Foundation. 2-3: Denver Public Library, Western History Department. 5: Rare Book and Special Collections Division, Library of Congress (LC).

MIGRANTS TO A NEW WORLD

Pages 8-9: Caribou, Alaska tundra, Helen Rhode. 10: Top, Arizona State Museum, University of Arizona. Below and 11, Rob McKenzie, courtesy of the Natural History Museum of Los Angeles County. 12: Bottom right, Henry Sheldon. 13: Smithsonian Institution. 14: Map by Jack Shepherd. 15: Top left, Warren Garst/Tom Stack and Associates. Bottom left, John S. Flannery. Right, D. H. Pimlott. 16-17: Ron Klataske. 17: Top, Carmelo Guadagno, Museum of the American Indian, Heye Foundation. Bottom, map by Davis Meltzer. 18-19: The John Rylands University Library of Manchester; 1854 facsimile edition of the *Desceliers Mappemonde*, Public Archives of Canada. 20: Top, Moll's *Map of North America*, Geography and Map Division, LC. Below, Duhamel du Monceau, *Traite Generale des Pesches*, Prints and Photographs Division, LC. 20-21: Bottom, *Book of St. Albans*, The Beinecke Rare Book and Manuscript Library, Yale University. 23: Top, *Codice Florentino*, courtesy of The American Museum of Natural History. 24, 25: David Muench.

EAST INTO A WILD EDEN

The pictographs and their translation appearing in Portfolio I are from the *Walam Olum or Red Score. The Migration Legend of the Lenni Lenape or Delaware Indians . . .* (Indianapolis: Indiana Historical Society, 1954), and published here with the permission of the Indiana Historical Society. The pictographs in *Walam Olum or Red Score* are from the manuscript in the hand of Constantine S. Rafinesque which is in the Brinton Memorial Library of the University Museum, University of Pennsylvania, and the translation is based on the Delaware words for the pictographs and their English meaning as recorded and translated by Rafinesque.

Maps appearing in the portfolio by Jack Shepherd. Page 27: Gift of Sir Edmund Osler, Royal Ontario Museum, Toronto, Canada. 28: Jaja Kopak, *Hunter Killing Bear*, Winnipeg Art Gallery, The Bessie Bulman Collection, photo by Tom Prescott. 29: Top left, courtesy of Charles Miles. Top right, courtesy of Donald Baird, Princeton University Museum of Natural History. 30 (top), 31, 32, and 33

(top): Carmelo Guadagno, Museum of the American Indian, Heye Foundation. 34: Top, George Catlin, *Buffalo Dance*, courtesy of Smithsonian Institution. 35: Top and bottom right, courtesy of Charles Miles. 35 (bottom left), 36, 37 (top), 38 (top), and 39 (top): Carmelo Guadagno, Museum of the American Indian, Heye Foundation. 39: Bottom, Abby Aldrich Rockefeller Folk Art Collection.

TAMING THE FOREST WILDERNESS

Pages 40-41: New Hampshire hardwood forest, Hallinan/FPG. 42-43: Santo Domingo Plate, Walter Bigges, *Expedition of Francis Drake* (Leyden, 1588) Classmark: *KB/†††/1588, Rare Book Division, The New York Public Library, Astor, Lenox and Tilden Foundations. 44: Left, Ashmolean Museum, Oxford. Top right, Benjamin West, *Colonel Guy Johnson*, National Gallery of Art, Andrew W. Mellon Collection, Washington. Bottom right, Erwin A. Bauer. 46-47: *The First Thanksgiving*, Pilgrim Hall Museum, The Pilgrim Society, Plymouth, Mass. 49: Top, *Wild Turkeys*, Museum of Comparative Zoology, Harvard University. Bottom left, George H. Harrison. 50: Top, Hudson's Bay Company. 51: Scott Swedberg. 52: Bottom left, *The Alegator of St. Johns*, Trustees of the British Museum (Natural History). 52-53 (center) and 53 (top right): James H. Carmichael, Jr. 54: *Natural History of Carolina, Florida, and the Bahama Islands*, Rare Book and Special Collections Division, LC. 55: Photos by Kenneth and Brenda Formanek. 56: Les Blacklock. 57: Top left, H. H. Cross, Prints and Photographs Division, LC.

PAINTERS OF A LUSH NEW LAND

Page 59: *A New Voyage to Carolina*, Rare Book and Special Collections Division, LC. 60-61: *The manner of their fishing, The broyling of their fish . . ., Towhee, A Land Tort*, reproduced by courtesy of the Trustees of the British Museum. 62-65: Rare Book and Special Collections Division, LC. 66: Top, American Philosophical Society. Bottom, and 67-69, Rare Book and Special Collections Division, LC. 70-71: *Viviparous Quadrupeds of North America*. The Beinecke Rare Book and Manuscript Library, Yale University.

WAGON WHEELS FOLLOW BUFFALO TRAILS

Pages 72-73: Nebraska grasslands, Entheos. 74: Bottom, American Philosophical Society. 74-75: Top, Ed Bry. 75: Bottom left, Dale A. Zimmerman. Bot-

tom right, American Philosophical Society. 76: Left, Larry Jay Roop. Top right, Joseph Van Wormer. Bottom right, Jim Yoakum. 78: Bottom, Leonard Lee Rue III. 78-79: Top, Karl Wimar, *Turf House on the Plains*, courtesy of The Bancroft Library. 79: Bottom, Robert E. Pelham. 80: Clark journals, Missouri Historical Society, St. Louis. 81: Top, Thomas Gilcrease Institute of American History and Art, Tulsa, Oklahoma. Bottom, Patrick Gass, *A Journal of Voyages and Travels of a Corps of Discovery*, Rare Book and Special Collections Division, LC. 82: Top and bottom left, Jen and Des Bartlett/Bruce Coleman Inc. Top and bottom right, Thomas Gilcrease Institute of American History and Art, Tulsa, Oklahoma. 84: Ed Park. 85: Karl Bodmer, *Dance Leader of the Hidatsa Dog's Society*, 1834. Warrior in the costume of the Dog Dance. From: Wiedneuwied, Maximilian. *Travels . . .* Atlas vol. copy 3. London, 1844. Plate 23. Classmark: *KF†††1844, Rare Book Division, The New York Public Library, Astor, Lenox and Tilden Foundations. 86: Top, The Beinecke Rare Book and Manuscript Library, Yale University. 86-87: Bottom, *Shooting Wild Pigeons in Iowa*, Prints and Photographs Division, LC. 87: Top, Robert Carr. 88: Bottom left, W. R. Leigh, *Sketch of Grey Wolf*, Thomas Gilcrease Institute of American History and Art, Tulsa, Oklahoma. Top right, Durward L. Allen. 88-89: Bottom, Wilford L. Miller.

LORD OF THE PLAINS

Page 91: American Philosophical Society. 92: Northern Natural Gas Company Collections, Josslyn Art Museum, Omaha, Nebraska. 93: Glenbow-Alberta Institute. 94-95: Courtesy, Amon Carter Museum, Fort Worth, Texas. 96-97: Bottom, *North American Indian Portfolio*, Rare Book and Special Collections Division, LC. 97: Top, Peter Rindisbacher "Buffalo and Prairie Wolves", *American Turf Register and Sporting Magazine*, July 1830 (vol. 1, no. 11) facing page 555, General Research and Humanities Division, The New York Public Library, Astor, Lenox and Tilden Foundations. 98: Top and bottom, Rare Book and Special Collections Division, LC. 99: Thomas Gilcrease Institute of American History and Art, Tulsa, Oklahoma. 100: Bottom, National Park Service: 100-01: Top, Smithsonian Institution. 101: Bottom, Thomas Gilcrease Institute of American History and Art, Tulsa, Oklahoma. 102: Courtesy of The R. W. Norton Art Gallery, Shreveport, Louisiana. 103: Northern Natural Gas Company Collections, Josslyn Art Museum, Omaha, Nebraska.

FRONTIER CLOSES

ges 104-05: Colorado Rockies, Nich-
deVore III/Bruce Coleman Inc. 106-
obert Belous. 108: William J. Weber.
Circus World Museum, Baraboo,
onsin. 110: Seal made by Jean Bol-
photo by Ron Bolton. 111: Joe Ry-
nik. 112: Bottom, Fred Bruemmer.
13: Top, Fish and Wildlife Photo-
h No. 22-HE-14 in the National
hives. 113: Bottom, Carleton Ray/
to Researchers, Inc. 114: Top, and
om left, Jeff Foott. Bottom right,
k journals, Missouri Historical So-
y, St. Louis. 116: Union Pacific Rail-
d Colorphoto. 117: Harry Engels.
-19: Top, Arlan R. Wiker. 119: Bot-
, Carmelo Guadagno, Museum of
American Indian, Heye Foundation.
: Top, reprinted by permission from
e Outlaw Gunner by Harry M. Walsh,
1971 by Tidewater Publishers, Cam-
dge, Md. Middle, Hearth and Home,
. 4, 1871, courtesy of Charles Scrib-
's Sons. Bottom, Millinery Trade Re-
w, 1901, published as cover photo of
ather Fashions and Bird Preservation
Robin W. Doughty, University of
alifornia Press, 1975, reprinted by per-
ission of the University of California
ess. 121: Michael Wotton.

LANDS OF WILDNESS

Small animal line drawings in port-
lio by Tina Bandle. Page 123: Acc. No.
58:53, Surveyor's Wagon in the Rockies
a. 1858, Albert Bierstadt, American,
830-1902, oil on paper mounted on can-
as, 7-3/4" x 12-7/8", gift of J. Lion-
berger Davis, courtesy of The St. Louis
Art Museum. 124: Courtesy, Hirschl and
Adler Galleries Inc., New York. 125: Bottom left, courtesy of National Collection
of Fine Arts, Smithsonian Institution.
Right, National Park Service. 126-27:

The Oakland Museum. 127: Top and
bottom right, National Park Service.
128-29: Courtesy of The Art Institute of
Chicago. 129: Bottom, U.S.D.I.—Na-
tional Park Service. 130: Top left, U.S.
Geological Survey. Bottom, J. W. Powell,
Canyons of the Colorado, LC. 131: Jeff-
erson National Expansion Memorial.
132: Courtesy of the Cooper-Hewitt Mu-
seum of Decorative Arts and Design,
Smithsonian Institution. 133: Top, oil on
canvas, 19"x29", given in memory of
Elias T. Milliken by his daughters, Mrs.
Edward Hale and Mrs. John Carroll
Perkins, 43.134, courtesy Museum of
Fine Arts, Boston. Bottom left, National
Park Service. 134: Top, Hawaii State
Archives. 134-35: Courtesy of The Amer-
ican Museum of Natural History.

THE TIDE TURNS

Pages 136-37: New Jersey marsh,
Grant Heilman. 139: Prints and Photographs Division, LC. 140 (top, and bottom left) and 140-41 (bottom): U.S. Forest Service. 141: Top, Jerry Wayne Davis.
142: Top, Les Blacklock. Bottom, William T. Bryson. 143: Dexter F. Landau.
144: Martin Bovey, Jr. 145: Top, Soil
Conservation Service—U.S.D.A. Bottom, Grant Heilman. 146: Thase Daniel.
147: Smithsonian Institution. 148: Top,
Des Moines Register and Tribune Company. Bottom, James C. Vincent. 149:
J. N. "Ding" Darling Foundation. 150-51:
Grant Heilman. 151: Right, Joan Stor-
month Black. 153: Top, Ed Dodd. Bottom, George H. Harrison.

TRIUMPHS OF CONCERN

Page 155: National Park Service. 156-
57: National Wildlife Federation. 158:
Laboratory of Ornithology, Cornell University, from Louis Agassiz Fuertes and
the Singular Beauty of Birds, F. G.

Marcham, Ed., Harper & Row Publish-
ers. 159: Ned Smith. 160: N.W.F. 161:
Ned Smith. 162: By John Clymer. 163: By
Guy Coheleach, 1972, courtesy of Frame
House Gallery, Inc., Louisville, Kentucky,
© 1972. 164: Clark Bronson. 165: Top,
Douglas Allen (1967) courtesy of Dr. and
Mrs. William Morton. Bottom, N.W.F.
166-67: Edward J. Bierly.

AN ENDURING PLACE FOR WILDLIFE

Pages 168-69: Gulls, northern Califor-
nia coast, David Muench. 170: Top, Tom
Myers. Bottom, Eugene A. Shinn. 171:
Russell Munson. 172-73 (bottom) and
173 (middle): R. H. Russell. 173: Top,
David Hiser. 175: Top, Whaling Scene,
1892, reproduced by courtesy of the New
York Historical Association, Coopers-
town, New York. Bottom left and right,
The Sea Library/Peter Lake. 176: Dar-
win Van Campen. 177: Top, Ed Farmer.
Bottom, Willis Peterson. 178: Top, Jack
Richard—Cody. Bottom, left, Don El-
sing. Bottom right, L. David Mech.

WILDLIFE IN OUR LIVES

Page 181: Ray Atkeson. 182: Top,
Luther Goldman. Bottom, left and right,
George H. Harrison. 183: E. P. Haddon.
184: Donna K. Grosvenor. 185: Top and
bottom, George H. Harrison. 186: Top
left, Grant Heilman. 186-87: Bottom,
Ted Trueblood. 187: Top, from High on
the Wild with Hemingway by Lloyd R.
Arnold. 188: Donald R. Nelson. 189:
Top, photo: Jerry Greenberg. Bottom,
Flip Schulke—Black Star. 190: Top,
George H. Harrison. Bottom, Ernest
Braun. 191: Grant Heilman.

APPENDIX

Page 192: U.S. Fish and Wildlife Service. 195-96: Maps by Janice Hawkins and
Jack Shepherd.

BIBLIOGRAPHY

Allen, Durward L. Our Wildlife Legacy. rev. ed. New York: Funk and Wag-
nalls, 1962.

Bakeless, John. The Eyes of Discovery.
N.Y.: Dover Publications, Inc., 1961.

Bradford, William. Mourt's Relation:
Or Journal of the Pilgrims in New
Plymouth. 1622. Edited by D. B. Heath.
New York: Corinth Books, 1963.

Chittenden, Hiram M. The American
Fur Trade of the Far West. 2 vols. N.Y.:
The Press of the Pioneers, Inc., 1935.

Dary, David A. The Buffalo Book.
Chicago: Sage Books, 1974.

DeVoto, Bernard. The Journals of
Lewis and Clark. Boston: Houghton
Mifflin Company, 1953.

Dorst, Jean. Before Nature Dies. Boston: Houghton Mifflin Company, 1970.

Farb, Peter. The Land and Wildlife of
North America. Life Nature Library.
New York: Time Incorporated, 1966.

Leopold, Aldo. A Sand County Almanac. New York: The Oxford University Press, 1966.

Lorant, Stefan. New World. rev. ed.
New York: Duell, Sloan and Pearce, 1965.

Matthiessen, Peter. Wildlife in America. New York: The Viking Press, 1959.

Milne, Lorus and Margery. Paths
Across the Earth. New York: Harper and
Row Publishers, Inc., 1958.

Monaghan, Jay, ed. The Book of the
American West. New York: Julian Mess-
ner, Inc., 1963.

Morison, Samuel Eliot. The Oxford
History of the American People. New
York: Oxford University Press, 1965.

Morton, Richard L. Colonial Virginia.
Vol. 1. Chapel Hill: University of North

Carolina Press, 1960.

Sandoz, Mari. The Beaver Men, Spear-
heads of Empire. New York: Hastings
House, 1973.

Savage, Henry Jr. Lost Heritage. New
York: William Morrow and Company,
Inc., 1970.

Smith, Henry Nash. Virgin Land. Cambridge: Harvard University Press, 1973.

Snell, Tee Loftin. The Wild Shores,
America's Beginnings. Washington, D.C.:
The National Geographic Society, 1974.

Trefethen, James B. Crusade for Wildlife. A Boone and Crockett Club Book.
Harrisburg: The Stackpole Co., 1961.

Walker, Ernest P. Mammals of the
World. 3rd rev. ed., 2 vols. Baltimore and
London: The Johns Hopkins University
Press, 1975.

Webb, Walter Prescott. The Great
Plains. N.Y.: Grosset and Dunlap, 1931.

National Wildlife Federation

1412 16th St., N.W.
Washington, D.C. 20036

Thomas L. Kimball, *Executive Vice President*
J. A. Brownridge, *Administrative Vice President*
James D. Davis, *Director, Book Development*

Staff for this Book

Russell Bourne, *Consulting Editor*
Alma Deane MacConomy, *Editor*
Jennifer Connor, *Art Editor*
Patricia Towle, *Research Editor*
Leah Bendavid-Val, *Permissions Editor*
Mel Baughman, *Production and Printing*

Acknowledgments

The editors felt fortunate to have at their disposal the lifetime learning and perspective of Dr. Raymond E. Johnson, recently retired director of research at the U.S. Fish and Wildlife Service. As wildlife consultant, he contributed ideas as well as facts from preliminary research through final editing of this history's many facets. We enjoyed working again with book designer Charles O. Hyman and with David F. Robinson who wrote the six portfolio essays, and we welcomed to NWF books Bruce Holloway whose interpretative line drawings of animals enrich the chapter illustrations.

While the editors received generous assistance from many NWF colleagues, including the editors of *National Wildlife, International Wildlife,* and *Ranger Rick's Nature Magazine,* we wish to acknowledge in particular the contributions of Louis S. Clapper, Kenneth R. Hampton, and George Reiger. Special thanks are also due to Natalie Rifkin who defined the idea for this bicentennial volume and did the editorial work on the portfolio "Triumphs of Concern."

Among many other individuals who were of invaluable help in the development of this book, the editors are particularly grateful to Linda Austin, Amon Carter Museum of Western Art; Charles Denny and David M. Hopkins, U.S. Geological Survey; John S. Gottschalk, International Association of Fish, Game and Conservation Commissioners; Carmelo Guadagno, Museum of the American Indian, Heye Foundation; Julia E. Harty, Rare Book and Special Collections Division, Library of Congress; Bob Hines, U.S. Fish and Wildlife Service; Carolyn Milligan, American Philosophical Society; John P. Russo, State of Arizona Game and Fish Department; Dennis Stanford and Beryl Simpson, Smithsonian Institution; Louise Walker, St. Louis Art Museum; and Marjorie Wynne, The Beinecke Rare Book and Manuscript Library, Yale University.

Generous assistance was also forthcoming from wildlife biologists, foresters, geologists, entomologists, cartographers, librarians, historians, and other specialists in the Army Center of Military History; Audubon Naturalist Society; Bureau of the Census; Bureau of Land Management; Energy Research and Development Administration; Environmental Protection Agency; Fairfax County, Virginia Library System; National Park Service; Patuxent Wildlife Research Center; President's Council on Environmental Quality; Smithsonian Institution; U.S. Fish and Wildlife Service; and the U.S. Forest Service.